COURTS AND THE POOR

COURTS AND THE POOR

CHRISTOPHER E. SMITH
THE UNIVERSITY OF AKRON

Nelson-Hall Publishers
Chicago

Cover Painting: *Floodgate II,* by John Ridlon

Library of Congress Cataloging-in-Publication Data

Smith, Christopher E.
  Courts and the poor / Christopher E. Smith.
    p.   cm.
  Includes bibliographical references and index.
  ISBN 0-8304-1296-4.—ISBN 0-8304-1227-1 (pbk)
    1. Courts—United States.   2. Equality before the law—United
States.   3. Legal assistance to the poor—United States.
4. Justice, Administration of—United States.   I. Title.
KF8700.S585   1991
347.73′1—dc20
[347.3071]   90-48086
                                                                    CIP

Manufactured in the United States of America

10 9 8 7 6 5 4 3 2 1

The paper used in this book meets the
minimum requirements of American
National Standard for Information
Sciences—Permanence of Paper for
Printed Library Materials, ANSI
Z39.48-1984.

For my parents,
Carol Payne Smith
and
Robert L. Smith

Contents

Preface

Social science research on the judicial system has blossomed since the 1960s. Earlier academic literature on the judiciary tended to focus almost exclusively upon the jurisprudential theories and legal opinions enunciated by judges. During the past three decades, however, the application of social science theories and methods has enabled scholars to shift their attention from the rules of law to the processes and outcomes generated by legal institutions. Rather than continuing to assume that courts are governed by formal legal rules and procedures, analysts discovered the subtle political influences and processes that actually determine judicial outcomes. Recognition of the complex political and social factors that influence the judiciary made it possible for analysts to study and question the human consequences of procedures and decisions within the court system. In theory, the application of neutral laws will lead to equal justice for all citizens. In reality, however, the inherently political nature of the judicial system insures that certain individuals and interests will enjoy greater advantages and benefits in their contacts with courts and law.

This book attempts to bring together the accumulated social science and legal scholarship on the judiciary in order to examine wealth discrimination, a primary source of advantages and disadvantages for individuals within the judicial process. Although people recognize that wealthy individuals enjoy certain advantages in utilizing the legal system, the extent of affluent people's advantages in each stage of the judicial process is not easily discernible by the outside observer. Contemporary social science research provides the means through which wealth discrimination can be documented throughout the judicial system.

Previous books and articles examining wealth discrimination focused primarily upon either legal decisions affecting poor people or the individual stages in the judicial process in which less affluent people suffer detrimental consequences. This book is relatively unusual in its attempt to present a comprehensive picture of wealth discrimination by combining the preceding approaches to examine the various stages of the judicial process as well as court cases affecting the poor. The final chapters of this book draw from two additional important areas of judicial research, namely judicial policy making and comparative legal studies, which are often treated (or ignored) as separate subjects. Hopefully this effort to utilize and integrate all of the major subjects of judicial and legal scholarship has succeeded in illuminating the problems of wealth discrimination as well as the possibilities for reform.

Although my own analyses and arguments are evident throughout this book, I relied extensively upon the work of other scholars who study the judiciary. As with any endeavor seeking to integrate and expand a body of scholarly literature, I obviously owe a great debt to the many political scientists, sociologists, legal scholars, and criminologists who have questioned, studied, analyzed, and described various aspects of law and the judicial system. I am especially grateful for and impressed by the work of the scholars who are active in the Law and Society Association. In its role as the interdisciplinary connecting point for scholars from a variety of fields, the Association, through its members, has made immeasurable contributions to judicial research. This scholarly research has greatly enhanced the arguments and evidence presented in the chapters that follow.

I am very grateful to the people who assisted me in producing this book. I owe a special debt to my father, Robert L. Smith of Western Michigan University, for his editorial advice and assistance on the final manuscript. Several friends and colleagues generously gave their time to read and comment on portions of the manuscript: Stephen Brooks and Carl Lieberman of the University of Akron, George Cole of the University of Connecticut, and Ronald Kramer of Western Michigan University. Bonnie Ralston and Mari Bell Nolan provided their usual outstanding assistance in the preparation of the final manuscript.

As always, my wife, Charlotte, and my daughter, Alicia, provided the necessary support and patience to permit timely completion of this project.

This book is dedicated to my parents, Carol Payne Smith and Robert L. Smith. In addition to providing substantial support and guidance for my personal and professional development, they have served as my role models as educators and social activists. Recognition of my parents' accomplishments as catalysts for social change in their local community has probably been lost to history as society gradually has moved toward their egalitarian viewpoints about racial and gender equality. Within their respective spheres of professional influence, namely education and theater, each of them took risks and endured opposition in breaking down established discriminatory barriers during the 1960s and 1970s. Today, in their roles as professors at Western Michigan University, they both continue to raise their students' and colleagues' consciousness about issues of equality.

CHAPTER ONE

Courts and Affluence in American Society

A merican society contains a complete spectrum of wealth, from affluent people enjoying the lifestyles of the rich and famous to destitute homeless people living in the streets. Anyone in the United States, regardless of their income, can enter the court system. Some people are dragged into court by being arrested for violating criminal laws while others voluntarily seek judicial assistance by filing lawsuits. The American legal system is supposed to apply the same rules and procedures to all people. Inscribed in large letters above the entrance to the Supreme Court of the United States are the words "Equal Justice Under Law." These words represent the aspirational ideal of the American judicial system, namely that law and legal procedures will treat people equally regardless of their race, gender, religion, or social status. Because the judiciary portrays itself as providing impartial decisions, it deserves close scrutiny to determine the extent to which legal principles and court procedures achieve the aspirational ideal of equal justice. Unlike the legislative and executive branches, in which wealthy and organized interests obviously receive preferential treatment because of their lobbyists and campaign contributions, the pervasiveness of wealth discrimination is less apparent in the components of American law and judicial process.

Expectations about Judicial Neutrality

Americans have mixed expectations about the operation of government. On the one hand, citizens want government agencies to fix roads, provide Social Security assistance, and plan for the nation's economic and military needs. These daily demands for services are balanced, on the other hand, by a degree of public cynicism about the political maneuvering that underlies the development of governmental policies. Interest group politics, negative campaigning, and periodic scandals in defense procurement and other programs reinforce the view that the legislative and executive branches of government are influenced by egomania, greed, and partisanship among politicians and bureaucrats. The political nature of these branches is evident in the calculated promises and cautious public posturing of elected officials.

Although Ronald Reagan tapped this public skepticism about government to win two presidential elections, his administration's scandals in such agencies as the Department of Housing and Urban Development and the Environmental Protection Agency simply perpetuated the role of partisanship and self-interest in the political branches of government. In the aftermath of the Reagan era, commentators have raised questions about the possibility of effective government.[1] Elected officials appear to lack the political courage to move beyond special-interest politics and safe, symbolic statements about lowering taxes and saluting the flag in order to tackle difficult issues such as the federal budget deficit.

By contrast, the judiciary is viewed differently as a branch of government. Citizens presume that the courts are unencumbered by the naked partisanship that permeates other governmental arenas. Although people recognize that policies which develop in the legislative and executive branches are influenced by politics, they carry an expectation that the judiciary is governed by law and therefore, unlike the other branches, is not guided by money and politics. Indeed, the symbols and language of law utilized in the judiciary attempt to reinforce an image of neutrality and objectivity. As described by Harry Stumpf, the judiciary seeks to reassure the citizenry that judicial outcomes are determined by law and not by politics:

> With symbols such as law degrees, robes, walnut-paneled courtrooms, elevated benches, a special language, and the like, we help sustain the myth of an impersonal judiciary divining decisions based on some objective truth contained in the Constitution (another symbol), and knowable only by a select few. It is all a very reassuring view of policy-making (or rather, rule divining), for after the tumult, greed, and indecisiveness of the legislative process—not to mention the excesses, embarrassments and dissonance of the executive policy process—we quickly weary of the frustrations and disappointments of plain old POLITICS and wish to repair to the serenity, the sureness, indeed the utter sublimity of JUSTICE, which the LAW and its purveyors promise.[2]

These expectations about neutrality apply to each of the important functions that courts perform for society.[3] The judicial system provides a forum in which disputes can be structured and processed according to established rules and fair procedures. Thus, conflicts and disagreements can be shaped, managed, and processed without disrupting society. Criminal courts exercise society's power to punish citizens in order to modify undesirable behavior. Courts also distribute gains and losses in society by ordering compensation for injured people, determining ownership of corporate or personal property, and making other decisions that allocate resources. Court decisions can determine governmental policies in education, housing, employment, and other important areas of public policy. In all of these functions, there is an expectation that courts should be open and equally receptive to the legitimate claims of any citizens. Because any individual, regardless of race or social status, can initiate a legal action, the judicial system is structured to hear and respond to the arguments of the lone individuals and powerless groups who are easily ignored elsewhere in government.

The imagery of law and justice within courts obscures the way by which the judicial process yields distinctly unequal opportunities and results. Because courts are actually political institutions comprised of human beings with values and interests, the judicial system falls short of its idealized image. For example, although most judges are well-intentioned and strive for objectivity and neutrality, because they are fallible human beings, their decisions are inevitably influenced by their personal experiences and beliefs. Other actors, such as prosecutors, defense attorneys, and jurors, are similarly influenced by their attitudes and personal interests. Because judicial actors make subjective, discretionary decisions that determine case outcomes, there are always risks of discriminatory results for various individuals and groups. In the chapters that follow, this book will discuss the various ways, both obvious and subtle, in which law and judicial procedures lead to detrimental outcomes for less affluent people.

Poverty and Affluence in the United States

The existence of broad disparities in the distribution of income and wealth is a continuing feature of American society. In 1987, 32.5 million people, comprising over 13 percent of population, had incomes which placed them below the government's poverty line.[4] This represented an increase of 8 million people over the poverty population in 1978. Although the number and percentage of people in poverty declined from 1983 to 1987, both figures remained well above the levels for the 1970s. The percentage of Americans living in poverty decreased dramatically from 22 percent to 12 percent during the 1960s, but rose sharply again in the early 1980s.[5] These figures verify the continuing existence of millions of Americans who lack the resources to provide for the basic necessities in life.

The causes and extent of poverty in the United States are subject to controversy. During the 1980s, some authors claimed that government social welfare programs established in the 1960s worsened the economic status of the poor.[6] Others argued that there really is no poverty in America when compared to "real" poverty in countries with famines and a complete absence of modern technology.[7] These political viewpoints undoubtedly contributed to the trend in the 1980s of reduced governmental assistance for the poor. For example, between 1981 and 1988, $3.6 billion and 440,000 families were cut from Aid to Families with Dependent Children and federal funds for public housing were reduced from $32 billion to $6.5 billion.[8] These cutbacks affected the increased numbers of people living below the government poverty line during the 1980s. The reduction in attention to the plight of the poor by legislative and executive actors may increase expectations that the judiciary, as the supposedly impartial branch of government, will safeguard the interests of this politically powerless minority.

Scholars now recognize that poverty has spread from the central cities to many suburbs. For example, per capita income figures for Chicago's suburbs illustrate the gap between rich and poor in that metropolitan area. The $61,950 per capita income in the suburb of Kenilworth is nearly thirteen times greater than the $4,493 per capita income in suburban Ford Heights.[9] From 1979 to 1987, the adjusted income of people in the bottom fifth of American society declined by 10 percent. By contrast, during the same period, the wealthiest fifth of American society saw its income increase by 16 percent.[10] Despite arguments about how to define or control poverty, it is clear that disparities in the distribution of wealth are increasing.

In this book, references to the "poor," "indigent," and "less affluent people" are not limited to those included in governmental definitions of the poverty population. The federal government's definition of the poverty line is both low and relatively arbitrary and therefore cannot purport to identify all people who must struggle to make ends meet. The government poverty level for a family of four in 1987 was $11,611.[11] However, because the costs of housing and other living expenses are so high in large cities, frequently $500 or more for a two-bedroom apartment, millions of people whose incomes exceed the poverty line must struggle to pay their bills. For example, 1.8 million four-member families had incomes between $10,000 and

$20,000 in 1986.[12] Although most of these families were above the government poverty level, they would have a difficult time purchasing a home and making car payments, let alone paying attorneys to pursue litigation or finding bail money if they were arrested for a criminal offense. Millions of other people in families of varying sizes are also above governmental poverty definitions but too poor to enjoy adequate resources for effective participation in judicial proceedings.

Although some chapters will include specific references to people below governmental poverty levels, other sections will speak more generally about less affluent people who lack the necessary disposable income to pay for attorneys' fees, litigation expenses, and other costs associated with participation in the judicial process. Because nearly 42 percent of America's 64.5 million families had incomes below $25,000 in 1986, there are obviously millions of Americans who have limited available resources.[13] By contrast, 32 percent of American families had incomes in excess of $40,000 in 1986, well above the median family income of $29,458.[14] These individuals, as well as corporations and other business enterprises, enjoy greater opportunities to take full advantage of the courts' functions for dispute processing, resource allocation, and policy-making.

Because less affluent people lack the resources and organizations to influence the legislative and executive branches through lobbyists and political action committees, the courts bear a special responsibility for safeguarding the rights of these relatively powerless individuals. As subsequent chapters will discuss, however, legal doctrine and court processes can significantly disadvantage poor people who seek to pursue claims.

Race and Poverty

Contrary to a common stereotype depicting most poor people as members of racial minority groups, most Americans who live in poverty are white. However, because only 66 percent of the people living below the government's poverty line are white, racial minorities, who comprise just over 15 percent of the population, are clearly overrepresented, in that they constitute 34 percent of the poor.[15] The disproportionate economic disadvantages experienced by racial minorities are a continuing legacy of America's history of slavery and institutionalized discrimination.

Despite the elimination of many formal barriers to equal opportunity through antidiscrimination legislation and court decisions, the consequences of racial discrimination remain evident in poverty statistics. As several scholars demonstrated in a 1988 book edited by

Fred Harris and Roger Wilkins, poverty and unemployment among racial minorities became more persistent and severe during the 1970s and 1980s.[16] During the 1970s, the decline of American industry and the loss of relatively high-paying unionized manufacturing jobs exacerbated these conditions. Many blue-collar workers became unemployed or were forced into lower paying jobs in service industries.

Efforts to reduce the legacy of racial discrimination through affirmative action programs increased educational and employment opportunities for some minority group members. In fact, the economic gains made by middle-class minority group members led William J. Wilson, in his famous book *The Declining Significance of Race*, to argue that social class rather than race is the most important determinant of opportunity and success in American society.[17] Because most equal opportunity programs are focused upon higher education, government employment, and white-collar jobs, many poor people lack the necessary education and skills to benefit from such programs. As Wilson notes, "affirmative action programs are not designed to deal with the problem of the disproportionate concentration of blacks in the low-rate labor market."[18]

Because many government officials do not regard the advancement of equality as an important policy goal, the prospects for aggressively addressing the legacy of racial discrimination remain dim. Although officials in the Reagan administration reduced enforcement of civil rights laws and devoted the federal government's legal resources to fighting against existing laws to advance equality, they were not completely successful in efforts to eliminate antidiscrimination laws and affirmative action programs.[19] In 1989, however, Reagan-appointed justices to the United States Supreme Court formed a new majority that altered case precedents by curtailing affirmative action programs[20] and limiting the scope of well-established employment discrimination laws.[21]

For most of the history of the American judicial system, discretionary decisions by police, prosecutors, judges, and juries helped to perpetuate the oppression of minorities. For example, until the 1960s, juries in southern states would rarely convict a white person for committing a crime against an African-American, regardless of the strength of the evidence. The eventual reduction in overt racism did not completely eliminate detectable discriminatory effects. A significant literature of scholarly studies and governmental reports discusses the continued existence of racial discrimination in the judiciary.[22] In 1989, for example, two reports commissioned by the Michigan Supreme Court documented the persistence of discrimination by race as well as gender within the Michigan court system.[23] As recently as 1987, the United States Supreme Court has been confronted with sophisticated statistical evidence demonstrating that racial discrimination influences the imposition of the death penalty.[24] The victims of discrimination are frequently poor as well as members of minority groups. Thus discussions of wealth discrimination will inevitably overlap with issues of racial discrimination. Because it is impossible to separate racial discrimination from wealth discrimination in all circumstances, analyses of laws and judicial procedures must include a recognition that racial bias may contribute to discernible discriminatory effects against the poor.

The Capabilities of Courts

Stuart Scheingold has documented how politically powerless groups possess optimism and naive faith about the possibilities for judicial action to redress social injustice.[25] According to Scheingold, this reassuring "myth of rights" leads people to believe that judicial action is available and effective for overcoming disadvantageous policies and programs emanating from the political branches of government. In the aftermath of the Supreme Court's civil rights decisions of the 1950s and 1960s, various disadvantaged political minorities, including poor people, looked to the courts as a powerful source of protection and vindication.

The pervasive "myth of rights" is reinforced by conceptualizations of courts as effective policy making forums. In one well-known depiction of judges' capabilities for addressing significant public policy issues, Abram Chayes provided a variety of reasons to regard courts as good forums for policy making.[26] According to Chayes, judges have a professional tradition of neutrality; courts provide all interested parties with opportunities to present evidence and arguments; courts provide nonbureaucratic decision making; and courts can tailor *ad hoc* solutions for specific problems.

By contrast, in his well-known book *The Courts and Social Policy*, Donald Horowitz argues that courts lack the capability to make and implement policies effectively.[27] Horowitz asserts that judges lack the expertise to make difficult policy decisions. In addition, judicial policies tend to address unrepresentative problems in specific cases rather than the larger, underlying societal issues. He also notes that adversarial litigation creates incentives to hide and distort information rather than to provide the decision maker with a complete basis for making an appropriate judgment.

Which view of courts is correct? Courts obviously have some capability to go against the political *status quo* by issuing decisions on controversial issues. School desegregation and criminal defendants' rights provide examples of issues in which judicial decisions changed the nation's policies in spite of opposition from the elected branches of government. These noteworthy decisions do not imply, however, that the everyday operations of the judiciary are compatible with the idealized conception of courts embodied in the myth of rights and Chayes' view of judges as effective policymakers. For many cases, Horowitz's views usefully illuminate the ways in which actual court practices do not live up to idealized expectations.

An underlying theme of this book is that although courts may sometimes initiate policies and vindicate rights for political minorities, judicial processes do not fit idealized conceptions of neutrality and equal justice. Court processes and judicial decision making are guided by the same kinds of factors, namely discretion, resource scarcity, and exchange relationships, that influence outcomes in other political institutions. For example, many individuals cannot gain access to courts because of the costs, both financial and personal, of pursuing litigation. In other words, they lack the necessary resources to make effective use of the judicial branch of government. In addition, decision makers within courts, including attorneys and prosecutors as well as judges, exercise discretion based upon their attitudes, values, and beliefs. It is these discretionary decisions, rather than neutral legal principles, that influence the outcomes of court cases. The application of well-established legal doctrine does not insure that judicial decisions achieve any abstract standard of justice. In fact, legal decisions actually reflect the subjective viewpoints and background experiences of the political elites who comprise the judiciary. Evidence of political factors affecting judicial outcomes can be found in sophisticated statistical studies of court decisions which indicate that factors such as political party affiliation and prosecutorial experience are associated with particular kinds of decisions in civil liberties cases.[28] Thus, instead of being directed toward consistent decisions according to supposedly neutral principles of law, judges can apply their discretion, according to their individual backgrounds, attitudes, and beliefs, to treat similar cases quite differently.

Contrary to idealized conceptions of judicial authority, judges frequently lack the practical political power to enforce their decisions. Judicial decisions are not self-executing. Judges can experience difficult problems in gaining the cooperation of officials in local government who must implement policy decisions.[29] Thus, even when judicial policies recognize claims by politically powerless people, such as the poor, the court decisions may be merely symbolic, supportive declarations because courts lack the ability to implement decisions effectively. The influence of political factors over judicial decision making and policy implementation indicates that courts are complex institutions contained within the governing political system rather than separate, impartial entities.

There is significant social science literature on the political factors that influence judicial proceedings.[30] In an effort to analyze the extent to which courts provide equal justice for less affluent people, this book draws from the accumulated research of legal scholars, sociologists, and political scientists that examines the actual consequences of judicial processes and law. Some of the studies generate analyses and conclusions based upon a researcher's personal observations of the behind-the-scenes processes within the judiciary.[31] Other studies utilize quantitative analysis to identify influential factors, such as litigants' social status and wealth, which may lead to unequal judicial outcomes.[32] Although some commentators have raised concerns about the desirability of applying social science research to judicial institutions,[33] there is no better tool for evaluating the actual consequences of legal doctrines and court processes. Empirical research provides the only basis for accurate judgments about the degree to which courts succeed or fail in pursuing the aspirational goal of neutrality and equal justice.

Judges and the Poor

As key decision makers determining judicial outcomes that affect less affluent people, judges provide an excellent illustration of political influences upon legal proceedings. Judges are drawn from highly educated political elites within society. For example, as of 1983, over 60 percent of President Reagan's district judge appointees had a personal net worth between $200,000 and $1 million and an additional 21 percent had assets exceeding $1 million.[34] The Reagan appellate appointees had even more money with over 26 percent in the millionaire category.[35] In all judicial selection systems, both state and federal, even though all judges are not wealthy, especially if they were previously government attorneys, nearly all have connections with political parties and interest groups which permit them to receive judicial appointments or win election to the bench. Judges' affluence and elite political connections can provide them with experiences and viewpoints about society different from those possessed by less affluent citizens whose lives are affected by judges' decisions.

Although some judges have risen from modest circumstances and impoverished backgrounds, because of their high social status and income, even these judges may lose touch with social forces affecting poor people in society. If established principles of law contained clear answers for legal questions, there would be little need for judges to be in touch with the daily lives of the general citizenry. Because law is flexible and changeable in the hands of judges, however, it is generally acknowledged that judges must have an understanding of society in order to make fair decisions. Chief Justice William Rehnquist, a jurist known for his deference to political majorities rather than for his sensitivity to powerless groups such as the poor, has noted the importance of judicial appointees possessing " 'common sense,' some patchwork of knowledge of the human condition gained from experience, or put some other way, the best judges undoubtedly have some sort of understanding of human nature and how the world works."[36] This recognition serves as an implicit admission that judicial decisions are not determined by neutral principles of law, but rather by the values and viewpoints of judges. Despite this acknowledgement of the need for judges to understand social conditions, judges frequently evince little understanding of life outside the courthouse and the elite strata of society.

For example, in a report submitted by federal judges to justify proposed salary increases, one judge was quoted anonymously saying: "The long term financial sacrifice for my family is too much. I cannot sentence them to a lifetime of genteel *poverty*" (emphasis supplied).[37] In a press conference concerning the same issue, Chief Justice Rehnquist manifested a similar insensitivity by asserting that judges are not paid enough to enable them to educate their children.[38] In fact, at the time these statements were made, federal judges earned at least $89,500.[39] This salary level was over three times the median family income in the United States and placed judges' incomes in the top 7 percent of all families in the country.[40] Judges' salaries moved even higher after congressional action in November 1989 to raise salaries by nearly 40 percent by 1991.[41] Rehnquist's statement reflected no understanding of the struggles experienced by the other 90 percent of his countrymen who earn less money and who also seek to educate their children. An analysis of federal judges' effort to obtain higher salaries highlighted the gap between judges and the rest of American society:

> For anyone earning at least $89,500 annually, a sum that is over four times greater than that of the median salary for full-time American workers, to speak about living in poverty is outrageous. This characterization not only ignores the fact that millions of Americans are unemployed, homeless, and lacking medical insurance, but it bespeaks an absence of sensitivity to the harsh realities of life in American society and

the undeniably privileged position enjoyed by citizens who receive the relatively high salaries of federal judges.[42]

The awareness that judges possess about life in American society and, in particular, about poor people is of great importance because of the scholarly studies demonstrating the effects of judges' attitudes and backgrounds upon their decisions.[43] If judges possess little understanding of the social forces and pressures affecting poor people, it is unlikely that they will accurately detect wealth discrimination which adversely affects less affluent people within the judicial process.

Courts and the Poor

Because of important Supreme Court decisions, the court system has made great strides toward removing formal barriers to racial and gender equality in the judicial process. Although several obvious wealth discrimination mechanisms have been changed through reforms such as the provision of defense attorneys for indigent criminal defendants, there has been inadequate judicial awareness and scholarly attention focused upon the problem of unequal treatment of less affluent people within the court system.

Wealth discrimination receives less scrutiny in part because, unlike race, there are few explicitly recognized prohibitions against such discrimination in the U.S. Constitution. In addition, Americans tend to accept distinctions according to wealth as earned or deserved differences between people and therefore natural components of the social order. Moreover, discrimination by race or gender, such as categorical exclusion of women from jury panels, is sometimes discernible with the naked eye. By contrast, wealth discrimination may be less obvious without careful study of judicial processes and outcomes over a large group of cases. By focusing on the important areas of judicial process, including criminal justice, civil litigation, administrative proceedings, Supreme Court decisions, and judicial policy making, subsequent chapters will examine the subtle and not-so-subtle effects of wealth discrimination within the American court system.

CHAPTER TWO

The Poor and the Criminal Justice System

For several decades, commentators have noted that poor people suffer from discriminatory treatment in the criminal justice system. In his classic study of race relations in the 1940s, Gunnar Myrdal documented many detrimental consequences for poor people drawn into the criminal court system. Myrdal observed that "[t]he American bond and bail system works automatically against the poor classes" and that when state prison systems need money, "the inclination is to fine Negroes and poor whites to reduce the burden of cost of the legal system."[1] In 1967, while working for the President's Commission on Law Enforcement and Administration of Justice, Patricia Wald, later to become a United States Court of Appeals judge, wrote that "[t]he poor are arrested more often, convicted more frequently, sentenced more harshly, rehabilitated less successfully than the rest of society."[2] During the 1960s, many criminologists began to examine criminal justice through the political conflicts within American society rather than by analyzing deviant behavior by individuals. These conflict-oriented theorists posited that:

> The lower class person is (1) more likely to be scrutinized and therefore to be observed in any violation of the law, (2) more likely to be arrested if discovered under suspicious circumstances, (3) more likely to spend time between arrest and trial in jail, (4) more likely to come to trial, (5) more likely to be found guilty, and (6) if found guilty more likely to receive harsh punishment.[3]

The purpose of this chapter is to assess the continuing vitality of these observations and theories in light of social science concepts and empirical research in subsequent decades. It is difficult to portray a complete picture of the differential treatment of poor people because, unlike the substantial academic literature on racial discrimination in the criminal justice system, there has been less systematic attention given to the consequences of individuals' socioeconomic status within judicial processes.

The Politics of Justice

Officials in the criminal justice system identify and process individuals suspected of violating criminal laws. The distinctive feature of criminal law, as opposed to other areas of law, is the application of the state's resources and coercive power to punish offenders. Because authoritative decisions by police officers, prosecutors, judges, and other actors within the criminal justice system can result in the harshest sanctions available within a free society, namely government-sponsored deprivation of liberty, property, or even lives, there is a special need for court processes to operate in an impartial, nondiscriminatory manner. As indicated earlier, the American democratic ideal that all people should receive equal and fair treatment by government is presumed to have extra importance in the judiciary. The aspiration for even-handed treatment of all individuals within the legal system is evident in the symbols of law visible at American courthouses, from the blindfolded goddess carefully balancing the scales of justice to the words "Equal Justice Under Law" etched prominently in marble at the top of the Supreme Court building. This aspiration remains unfulfilled, however, because courts are human institutions governed by people possessing specific values and interests.

Judicial actors are inevitably affected by the social and historical forces, including prevailing political interests and values, that shape and determine public policies. For example, legislative bodies that write laws affecting courts represent middle-class electoral majorities and are influenced by highly organized and well-financed political and economic interest groups. In addition, the lawyers and judges who interpret and apply the laws are generally drawn from the ranks of educated, affluent elites. Because poor people lack resources and political power, they are subject to discrimination and control by governmental operations over which they can exert little influence.

Criminal Laws and Criminal Behavior

The Poor and the Definition of Crimes

Criminal laws are defined by elected politicians within legislative bodies. Although some citizens wish to believe that criminal laws represent the rules of natural morality, in fact such laws and the punishments prescribed for offending those laws change according to the values and political interests represented in Congress, state legislatures, and city councils at any given moment in history. Citizens presume that criminal laws are aimed at deterring and punishing socially-harmful behavior, yet the definition of which behavior is sufficiently harmful to merit the application of punishment by the state is controlled by governmental actors who emerge from and respond to a changing political environment. In 1932, for example, the manufacture and sale of intoxicating liquors was illegal throughout the United States. However, with the ratification of the Twenty-First Amendment repealing Prohibition in December 1933, those same actions became legal although they were presumably as immoral and harmful as they had been the year before. The inherent qualities of the regulated behavior did not change, but the political interests and institutions defining permissible behavior had changed.

Because poor people lack political resources and influence within governmental institutions, the definition of criminal laws is within the hands of the decision makers representing the interests of the middle-class and the affluent. As a result, the definition and enforcement of some criminal laws can have especially detrimental impact upon the poor. For example, an important reason why alcohol is legal and marijuana is illegal is that despite the fact that both intoxicants are subject to abuse and cause significant medical and social harms, marijuana was the drug of choice for poor members of racial minority groups when it was declared illegal. According to a comprehensive study on narcotics regulation, "[c]lass consciousness was a recurrent element in mari[j]uana prohibition even in its infancy."[4] By contrast, alcohol consumption was and remains an accepted social behavior among the groups who possess political power and control governmental institutions.

In a more obvious example, the literature that emerged during the 1960s on ghetto life among poor African-Americans described examples of criminal sanctions and police harassment against participants in "numbers" games, privately-run, daily lotteries in which people placed small bets upon a selected number in the hope it would be that day's winning number. These inner-city lottery operations were the largest employers in some neighborhoods and provided loans to people within the community. According to Charles Silberman, "[i]n minority communities, too, numbers bankers . . . have been the major source of venture capital and long-term loans for aspiring businessmen and professionals."[5] Thus the gambling operations, defined as illegal by governmental institutions, provided many of the employment and financial resources for communities which were denied participation in those areas of mainstream society because of racial and socioeconomic discrimination. During the 1970s, however, state governments not only altered their positions on the legality of lottery gambling, they actually assumed control over the field and began using their own lotteries as a means of raising revenue. Instead of focusing resources upon enforcing sanctions against lottery participants, the state governments sought to gain for themselves the financial benefits that had previously gone to entrepreneurs within poor neighborhoods.

For a further example, one might look to crimes such as "public drunkenness" or "loitering." Although there are arguable justifications for such laws to protect against potential harms to people or property, virtually every concrete and identifiable harm is already covered by some other criminal law (e.g., assault, vandalism). In 1981, public drunkenness, disorderly conduct, and vagrancy accounted for 18.5 percent of all arrests, a percentage as great as the arrests for the serious crimes (i.e., homicide, rape, robbery, arson, etc.) recorded in the FBI's annual report on national crime rates.[6] John Irwin argues that the criminalization of a vague condition rather than a specific behavior provides the police with a discretionary tool to remove offensive social problems associated with the poor (i.e., alcoholism, hunger, homelessness) from the purview of more affluent citizens as they walk or drive down the street. The definition and enforcement of criminal laws may contribute to an "out of sight, out of mind" denial of the existence and extent of societal problems on the part of the affluent and politically dominant middle class.[7]

The existence of discriminatory aspects in the definition and enforcement of criminal laws does not imply that the interests of poor people are wholly different from those of other citizens with respect to the design of criminal justice laws and procedures. Because low-income households experience the highest rates of victimization from violent crimes and burglaries,[8] poor people's interests in preventing violent behavior and thefts coincide with those of all other citizens who desire order and stability in society. As subsequent sections will discuss, although there may be a consensus on the definition of many of these crimes, the discretionary judgments affecting enforcement of these laws lead to burdensome consequences for the poor.

Poverty and Criminal Behavior

There is substantial academic literature on the causes of criminal behavior.[9] Poverty is arguably a cause of crime because of limited opportunities for poor youngsters to succeed in mainstream society.

Alternatively, poor neighborhoods are claimed to suffer from increased violence as elements of community cohesion disintegrate with the departure of more successful families to the suburbs. From a more critical perspective, it has been asserted that the failures of the capitalist, free enterprise system have created unemployment and poverty which give rise to social disorder and crime and lead to repressive countermeasures by the controlling political elite. Other theories have attempted to link genetic factors with social factors to explain deviant behavior and its overrepresentation among the poor.

Frequently analyses of this issue are clouded by value-laden choices which selectively explore the causes of crime. For example, many discussions overlook the causes and extent of white-collar crimes and harmful acts by corporations which constitute the greatest economic loss to society and are committed by affluent people.[10] Analysts also ignore the prevalence of illegal actions by nearly all people, regardless of social status, as evidenced by studies indicating that over 90 percent of Americans have broken some criminal law.[11] As Samuel Walker has noted:

> The prisons are disproportionately black not primarily because of a racial discrimination in sentencing for particular crimes but because of a bias against crimes committed by lower-class persons. . . . Public policy does not give anything like the same emphasis to white-collar crimes, even though in dollar terms they cost us about ten times as much as all robberies and burglaries combined. . . . If all of our criminal statutes were enforced, . . . [p]risons would be filled with vast numbers of additional white offenders. The differential treatment given perpetrators of different types of crimes represents a form of discrimination based on social class. This is undoubtedly the most consistent pattern of bias within the criminal justice system.[12]

For the purposes of this book, rather than struggle with the complex and controversial issue of the relationship between poverty and criminal behavior, this chapter recognizes that poor people are overrepresented as suspects and offenders processed within the criminal justice system and examines the ways in which the actors and processes within the criminal justice system contribute to that overrepresentation.

The Criminal Justice System

Although we commonly refer to the police, prosecutors, judges, and other actors and institutions involved with criminal justice as comprising a "system," the term does not imply the existence of planning, coordination, and efficiency in the implementation of criminal laws. Significant fragmentation exists in criminal justice institutions and processes because various actors jealously guard their authority over separate responsibilities. There is relatively little coordination among the 19,691 separate local, state, and federal law enforcement agencies,[13] so the effects of police decision making and behavior upon poor people can vary dramatically from place to place. The term "system" is applicable as an appropriate conceptual framework for criminal justice institutions because, despite fragmentation, there are interdependent parts which must interact in order to achieve the goals of enforcing the criminal laws.

In George Cole's useful characterization, the criminal justice system is an open one with new cases, new personnel, and shifting political conditions affecting the environment in which criminal laws are implemented. Moreover, a state of scarcity exists in regard to time, money, information, and personnel which prevents the system's actors and institutions from processing every case according to formally prescribed criteria.[14] Thus, fewer than 10 percent of cases ultimately result in a formal jury trial, the final courtroom stage which usually fulfills the public's image for how courts are supposed to operate. Instead, the overwhelming majority of cases are terminated during earlier stages in the process through the discretion of police officers, prosecutors, and other actors. These officials decline to arrest, dismiss charges, bargain for guilty pleas, and otherwise conserve system resources and fulfill their own interests by filtering cases out of the system prior to trial.

Key Characteristics of the Criminal Justice System

Several characteristics of the criminal justice system can affect differential treatment of poor people within the system. First, actors throughout the system have a high degree of discretion in deciding if and how the criminal laws will be implemented within every situation that arises. At the first stage of the system, after the political institutions have defined the laws, police make decisions about whether or not to arrest people based upon departmental policies, situational pressures, and personal biases. During assaultive confrontations between spouses, for example, police officers frequently use their discretion to ignore criminal behavior (i.e., assault and battery). They seek to cool temporarily the combatants' tempers in what the officers may characterize as "merely" a domestic dispute. The decision to arrest in each situation can reflect a variety of factors: how the officers were treated by each spouse; the officers' views on how husbands should treat their wives; departmental policies on handling such situations; the officers' perceptions about the impact of an arrest upon the family; and even the amount of paperwork generated for the officer by a formal arrest.

Other actors in the system also have significant discretion in the daily decisions which determine the impact of the criminal justice system upon each individual. Because of the pervasiveness of discretionary decisions, it would be impossible to identify every situation in which personal biases and other factors might detrimentally affect the treatment of less affluent people. It is fairly easy, however, to cite a variety of examples to demonstrate how actors throughout the system exercise discretionary authority: deciding whether to drop charges (prosecutors), agreeing to provide bail money (bail bondsperson), determining sentences (judges), and enforcing prison disciplinary rules (correctional officers). The widespread and inevitable application of discretionary decisions weakens any formal decision-making criteria designed to encourage uniform treatment of defendants. The widespread use of discretion insures that inequities will exist.

Second, the existence of sequential tasks is another system characteristic which affects discretionary decisions because so many actors have decision-making authority over their own separate stages of the system. The decisions in one stage affect the decisions that can be made in later stages. If the police do not vigorously enforce laws against prostitution or other offenses, then the prosecutor cannot prosecute such cases. If the police and prosecutor vigorously pursue all possible offenders, then corrections officials may be forced to use their discretion to grant early releases in order to avoid overcrowding in prisons and jails. Because of the fragmentation, scarce resources, and self-interests of various actors within this system of sequential decisions, any attempt to eliminate discretion will simply move discretionary authority to some other stage in the system. For example, attempts to abolish prosecutors' discretionary decisions in plea bargaining can simply result in discretionary bargaining about charges at earlier stages in the process or sentence bargaining by judges at later stages.

Third, the widespread discretion and sequential tasks produce exchange relationships as interdependent actors cooperate to advance their own interests. As illustrated by Cole, "[a] judge's verdict in a felony case affects the arresting officer's record, the prosecutor's conviction rate, and the credibility of the probation officer's sentencing recommendation."[15] Thus, officials within the system need some degree of cooperation in order to be effective and their decisions are influenced by their anticipation of subsequent decisions by other actors in the sequential process.

Fourth, criminal justice officials are dependent upon others for resources. Police officers, prosecutors, judges, and other actors must be sensitive to the demands of legislators and the public in order to maintain resource support for themselves and the system. Because they are elected officials in most states, prosecutors and judges may risk their jobs if they act against public sentiments in processing highly publicized cases. These external influences may contribute to biased treatment of individual defendants if police, prosecutors, and judges bow to public opinion and other external political pressures.

These four important characteristics of the system, namely discretion, sequential tasks, exchange relationships, and resource dependence, affect the decisions made by criminal justice officials and can contribute to unequal treatment of individual citizens. The factors and their effects upon poor people can be illustrated by examining each stage of the criminal justice process beginning with the police, who typically provide the initial contact between citizens and the court system.

Law Enforcement

Historically, the police were a component of the prevailing political establishment. According to Samuel Walker, they "enforced the narrow prejudices of their constituencies, harassing 'undesirables' or discouraging any kind of 'unwelcome' behavior."[16] Not surprisingly, poor people were a focal point of police harassment and control. Walker notes, "To be sure, the poor, political radicals, blacks, and other people deemed 'undesirable' were victimized more often by police than other groups."[17] Although increased training and professionalism among law enforcement personnel diminished their roles as partisan political enforcers in many places, the 1960s brought a new crisis as all-white police in urban areas came to symbolize the continuing societal inequality that clashed with the rising expectations in poor, minority communities. According to Walker, "[t]he individual cop on the beat received the brunt of the anger of ghetto residents . . . [and] the cops themselves responded by seeing all of their critics as bomb-throwing militants."[18] In several cities, police actions were the direct cause of major riots during the 1960s. Rising crime rates, increasing expectations about civil rights, and federal court decisions affecting criminal justice processes heightened pressures upon law enforcement officials and contributed to the crisis in police-community relations.

Although desegregation of police departments and the increased political power of African-Americans within municipal governments have moderated some of the bases for conflict, the risks of distrust and discrimination against poor people remain. Several factors can contribute to detrimental treatment of less affluent people, including the history of conflict between the police and poor communities, the police role as enforcers of politically defined societal rules, and the discretionary decision-making authority vested in individual officers.

The Decision to Arrest

One of the most significant decisions made by law enforcement officers is the decision to arrest an individual and enter that person into the criminal justice processes which may lead to incarceration and other sanctions. As mentioned previously, police officers use their discretion to decide whether to arrest a suspected lawbreaker. In many situations, a police officer could ignore a violation, give a warning, or perceive the situation as requiring that individuals be steered away from the scene of a confrontation. In Michael Lipsky's terminology, police officers are "street-level bureaucrats" who represent the government in direct contacts with the citizenry, particularly in situations engendering hostile reactions and dangerous confrontations.[19] Most direct contacts between police officers and members of the public are in stressful circumstances in which someone is angry or upset and the officer is called upon to resolve the situation. As highly visible, uniformed symbols of the government, the police can easily become the available focal point for citizen dissatisfaction with government services or perceived injustices in society. In an environment of inadequate resources in which their authority is regularly challenged, police officers may apply their discretionary decisions either to avoid confrontation and maintain rapport with citizens or to assert their authority and demonstrate their control of situations.

Research on police officers' decisions to make arrests indicates that a variety of situational factors (e.g., witness complaints, seriousness of alleged offense) affect these discretionary decisions. The influence of these factors and the ultimate decision to arrest tend, however, to fall more heavily upon poor people. One study of police officers' decisions found that, although the police consider the seriousness of the alleged offense and the preferences of the victim in deciding whether or not to make an arrest, police "systematically apply more formal sanctions against persons in positions of social disadvantage."[20]

Other motivations also affect arrest decisions. Police will seek to demonstrate their authority by making arrests more frequently when they encounter antagonistic suspects or when there are bystanders observing the officers' interactions with the suspect.[21] These elements may have extra force in poor communities in which the police are the focal point for expressions of dissatisfaction about discriminatory treatment, police brutality, or the lack of government services. Police brutality is generally a response to challenges to an officer's authority,[22] and overreactions leading to disproportionate decisions to arrest poorer people may come from the same source.

The application of discretionary decisions by police can have similarly detrimental impacts upon suspected juvenile offenders. In an analysis of the data from Marvin Wolfgang and associates' classic study of all males born in Philadelphia in 1945,[23] there were clear indications that the police were more likely to send poor youths into the formal juvenile justice system rather than release them to their parents or refer them to a social services agency. This discrimination existed even when the sample of nine thousand cases was controlled for seriousness of offense and prior record, variables which are sometimes used to justify differential treatment of specific demographic groups within the criminal justice system. According to the study, "[a]t the levels of the police and the juvenile court, the low [socioeconomic status] subjects are treated consistently more severely than their counterparts, even when both legal variables [i.e., offense and record] are simultaneously controlled."[24]

Law Enforcement Strategy

Policy choices about where to deploy law enforcement personnel can have implications for the treatment of less affluent people. For example, James Q. Wilson and George Kelling have proposed that police be assigned to neighborhoods in order to focus efforts on maintaining order and strengthening citizens' perceptions of safety and calm. Their so-called "broken windows thesis" is based upon research in which cars abandoned in both poor and affluent neighborhoods were gradually vandalized and destroyed by passersby. Because Wilson and Kelling concluded that untended, disordered neighborhoods may encourage damaging and threatening behavior, they argued that police should concentrate on maintaining order and encouraging a sense of community in order to reduce both crime and the fear of crime. Although Wilson wants the police to "reinforce the informal control mechanisms of the community itself," there is a problem in defining the community standards to be maintained.[25] Who will decide what constitutes the values within a neighborhood? Because the police possess authority, it will naturally fall to them to make discretionary decisions. But can the middle-class police officer accurately decide whether a teenager's loud rap music on a "boom box" is a threat to the sense of order within a particular neighborhood? There are risks that the police officers will engender hostility by enforcing their own values and behavioral standards. Moreover, aggressive order-maintenance activities, especially those aimed at noncriminal behavior such as talking loudly or standing on a street corner, threaten Americans' expectations about personal freedom in everyday life.

According to Jerome Skolnick, police officers are "specifically *trained* to be suspicious, to perceive events or changes in the physical surroundings that indicate the occurrence or probability of disorder."[26] Because poor neighborhoods are frequently regarded as high-crime areas, police officers use their perceptions about individuals' social status to generate suspicions. In discussing the confusion of race and social class, Wilson has noted that poor people attract police attention as potential criminals who must be watched: "Because the urban lower class is today disproportionately black (just as it was once disproportionately Irish), a dark skin is to the police a statistically significant cue to social status, and thus to potential criminality."[27] This heightened suspicion and scrutiny of poor people as well as minority group members may contribute to their overrepresentation among people arrested by the police.

The police and other actors in the criminal justice system can also treat witnesses and victims differently when those people are poor. A study of decision making in criminal cases found that prosecutors frequently refused to pursue charges because of stereotyped perceptions of the victims. According to the researcher, the criteria used by prosecutors for assessing "good" victims and witnesses are frequently factors which favor middle-class people over those with less education and income: "A pleasant appearance, residence in a good neighborhood, a respectable job or occupation, lack of nervous mannerisms, and an ability to articulate clearly are decided advantages."[28] Police, who must make pivotal discretionary decisions about which cases to pursue, also bemoan the scarcity of "good" victims, although one researcher concluded that this potentially discriminatory criterion did not seem to affect police decisions within one New York City precinct.[29]

The allocation of police services is another area in which the poor may suffer discrimination because of their relative lack of political power. Because personnel allocation patterns frequently favor neighborhoods with the highest crime rates or most calls for service, some researchers have concluded that poor people do not suffer from discrimination in the distribution of police service resources. However, as Elinor Ostrom has noted, simple allocation of personnel does not indicate how the police are performing and if they are providing equitable services to poor neighborhoods.[30] Because of disagreements about the appropriate measures of service allocation, it is difficult to make empirically based judgments about the existence and extent of resource discrimination against poor neighborhoods. For example, surveys indicating negative citizen attitudes about the police in poor and minority communities have yielded a variety of alternative causal interpretations, including overt racial discrimination, excessive demands and expectations of people in poor neighborhoods, symbolic dissatisfaction with government in general, and problems in effectively communicating the needs of poor people to bureaucratic agencies. Ostrom's review of the literature on equity in police services shows the existence of dissatisfaction with police performance in poor and minority neighborhoods, but the sources and extent of these problems have yet to be clearly defined.

Bail and Jail

People who are arrested and charged with criminal violations face the possibility of sitting in jail for weeks or months if they cannot make bail. For lesser offenses, people may be released with merely a promise to appear at a future court hearing. For more serious infractions, bail is set by either the police or judicial officers depending upon the design of individual court systems. When the police set bail for misdemeanor offenses, the amount is usually drawn from an established schedule. When judicial officers set bail for more serious offenses, however, the amount of bail is frequently based upon a discretionary determination. In either case, poor people suffer disproportionately from a loss of freedom prior to trial, despite the judicial system's supposed adherence to the presumption of innocence until guilt is proven, because they lack the resources to gain pretrial release by posting bail. The usual amounts set for bail vary from city to city depending upon the political environment. For example, growth of political power among African-American politicians and the pressures from federal court decisions led to reform of abusive bail practices in Detroit.[31] In general, however, the essence of the bail system is captured in the title of one well-known study, *Freedom for Sale*.[32]

Traditionally, bail was intended to insure the appearance of the defendant at trial. It can also be utilized by judges for punitive purposes by setting bail so high that the defendant cannot gain release. Although the Eighth Amendment to the U.S. Constitution forbids "excessive bail," that term has not been clearly defined and there is no federal constitutional right to release before trial although some state constitutions grant a right to have bail set.

The Effects of Pretrial Detention

The consequences of failing to gain pretrial release can be significant. As Malcolm Feeley demonstrated in his aptly titled study of lower courts, *The Process Is the Punishment*, people who are processed through the criminal justice system, whether or not they are ultimately convicted, suffer a variety of punishments simply from being dragged through the process.[33] They must lose income-producing time from work in order to attend court appearances. In addition, while sitting in jail they may lose their jobs and their homes and suffer other detrimental consequences to their families' lives.

In studying the courts in three cities, James Eisenstein and Herbert Jacob found in Baltimore that over 38 percent of felony defendants were not released on bail and an additional 48 percent spent a week in jail prior to release. In Chicago the respective figures were 19 percent and 23 percent, and in Detroit, nearly 40 percent of the felony defendants did not gain pretrial release. Although many of the defendants ultimately had their cases dismissed or were acquitted (Detroit—40%, Baltimore—56%, Chicago—86%), the burdens on these defendants, most of whom were poor, were considerable:

> Many will not be able to remove the blemish of their arrest from police records despite the lack of conviction. Some are forced to spend time in pretrial detention. It is likely that the economic costs of these unsuccessful prosecutions are considerable (even if small in absolute terms for each defendant) because most of the defendants in felony cases come from the working poor or welfare families. In addition, there is considerable psychic cost to having the possibility of a long prison term hang over one's future for several weeks or months.[34]

In addition to suffering financial and personal costs from pretrial detention, defendants have less ability to assist in the preparation of their defenses. Moreover, jails are dangerous, depressing institutions which contain a continually changing population of criminal offenders, mentally ill people, and substance abusers. They also lack the recreational and other facilities which can keep prisoners occupied in prisons. The unconvicted poor defendants who are ostensibly presumed innocent lose the protections of many constitutional rights. For example, despite complaints from Justice Thurgood Marshall about disproportionate mistreatment of poor people who cannot afford release on bail,[35] the Supreme Court has allowed jail administrators to permit overcrowding within cellblocks and to conduct degrading body cavity searches without any basis for suspicion.[36] Perhaps more important than even the physical and financial harms from remaining in jail, studies indicate that failure to obtain pretrial release can increase the likelihood of conviction and the probability of a prison sentence.[37] While the middle-class defendant who can afford to make bail will reappear at trial well-dressed and accompanied by family and friends, the poor defendant who cannot make bail may be dragged into the courtroom wearing handcuffs and a prison jumpsuit. The imagery may affect judges and juries regardless of the evidence of guilt or innocence.

The inequities of the bail system are exacerbated by the pivotal role of a private, profit-seeking actor, the bail bondsperson. Defendants who cannot make bail can pay a bondsperson a 10 percent fee to provide the money for release. This private entrepreneur can decide which defendants to accept as clients and thereby can determine which individuals will gain release. Moreover, an affluent defendant who can afford bail will receive a refund of all or nearly all of the bail money paid directly to the court. By contrast, the poorer defendant loses 10 percent as the fee to the bondsperson. In addition, defendants who are dependent upon these private business people for pretrial release are at the mercy of collusive activities by bondspersons who refuse to accept certain defendants as clients in order to curry favor with the police or prosecutor.[38]

Efforts to reform the bail system in order to reduce the excessive burdens upon poor defendants were introduced in many cities. In New York City, for example, the Vera Institute developed and administered a program for interviewing and monitoring defendants in order to release people on their own recognizance and thereby avoid the imposition of money bail which inevitably results in jailing poor people. The program claimed to be successful in ensuring that defendants returned to court, and it was subsequently implemented in other cities. As Malcolm Feeley has shown, however, such reform efforts frequently failed to achieve their goals because the programs were not adequately evaluated and because actors within the criminal justice system were not committed to sustaining and institutionalizing the changed procedures.[39]

The Poor in Jail

A survey of jail inmates nationwide in 1978 demonstrated the extent to which poor people are disproportionately overrepresented in jail populations. Although 45 percent of male inmates had incomes below $3,000 for the previous year, only 15 percent of males in comparable age groups in the general population had incomes as low.[40] In 1986, 53 percent of the jail population had not been convicted of any crime.[41] The majority had been unable to afford bail and a small number had not had bail set. Irwin's study of the San Francisco jail revealed that jails are used by police as holding centers for society's problems.[42] People with mental illness or substance-abuse problems are frequently placed in jail because police seek to remove them from the streets and the authorities have few other places to send them. As described by Cole:

> Although popularized in folksong and in fiction, American jails have been called "the ultimate ghetto." Most of the more than 200,000 people in jails are poor. . . . Traditionally jails have been a dumping ground not only for the criminal but also for the public drunk, the mentally ill, the vagrant, and the moral deviant. Uniformly jam-packed and generally brutalizing, jails are almost never life-enhancing. They seem to be the oldest, most numerous, and most resistant to reform of all criminal justice processes and institutions.[43]

Although the overrepresentation of the poor in jails reflects the higher rates of violent and property crimes in many low-income neighborhoods, there are several factors within the criminal justice system which contribute to the discriminatory impact of pretrial incarceration. In particular, police officers' discretionary decisions to arrest have detrimental impacts upon the poor and the bail system's discriminatory characteristics contribute to disproportionate jailing of less affluent people.

Prosecution

Prosecutors are central figures in the processing of criminal defendants. Their discretionary decisions to dismiss charges or initiate more severe charges against defendants are not reviewable by any higher authority. As with the police, the application of unfettered discretion in determining who will be sent through the criminal justice system creates risks that bias will harm poor defendants. In addition, prosecutors make recommendations for setting bail and determining sentences and thereby help determine inmate composition in jails and prisons. Prosecutors' discretionary power can be applied to favor the interests of the wealthy and politically powerful by dismissing charges against those defendants while pursuing cases against other people. Because prosecutors are frequently elected officials, their decisions can be influenced by their desire to curry favor with voters or political elites. Poorer people whose electoral participation and political power are generally less than that of more affluent people may not receive the same attention and consideration in prosecutorial decisions.

Prosecutors' decisions are normally influenced by their desire to maintain relationships with other actors in the criminal justice system in order to ensure smooth and effective processing of cases.[44] For example, Eisenstein and Jacob have identified the operation of "courtroom workgroups" in which prosecutors, defense attorneys, and judges work together to achieve quick, efficient case processing through cooperative plea bargaining.[45] All of these courtroom actors possess shared goals and interests for processing cases efficiently. As a result, the majority of cases in criminal courts are administratively processed through discretionary dismissals and plea bargains. Only a few cases fit the model of complete adversarial trials protecting the rights of criminal defendants. From the perspective of poor defendants, the application of discretionary decisions by prosecutors as well as the cooperation between prosecutors and defense attorneys raise justifiable concerns about whether poor people are adequately represented. Because poor people frequently lack education and cannot afford to hire their own attorneys, there is a risk that the operations of the courtroom workgroup disadvantage less affluent people by pressuring them to accept plea arrangements that suit the interests of the judge, prosecutor, and appointed defense attorney.

Right to Counsel and Indigent Defense Systems

During most of America's past, criminal defendants had to pay for a lawyer if they wished to be represented in court. The right "to have assistance of counsel for his defense" contained in the Sixth Amendment of the U.S. Constitution simply meant that defendants had a right to have a defense attorney if they could afford one. As a consequence, criminal trials tended to be brief, one-sided confrontations in which the prosecutor presented evidence, the defendant said a few words in his own defense, and the judge imposed a sentence within a short period of time. Cases were tried so swiftly that courts could handle several trials each day. Obviously, poorer defendants were significantly disadvantaged in a system in which the existence of any legal representation was based upon ability to pay.

In 1938, the Supreme Court construed the Sixth Amendment right to counsel as requiring the appointment of lawyers to represent indigent defendants in federal cases.[46] At that time, however, the provisions of the Constitution's Bill of Rights were not regarded as applying to state criminal justice systems so the majority of defendants charged with violating state laws remained unrepresented if they could not afford to hire counsel themselves. Gradually, the Supreme Court recognized circumstances in which the inherent unfairness of the courtroom mismatch between professional prosecutors and poor, uneducated defendants required that states provide lawyers for indigent defendants. For example, in the famous Alabama case of the "Scottsboro boys" in the early 1930s, several young African-American men, who were not represented by lawyers, were given death sentences after a hurried trial in which they were convicted of raping two white women—based upon testimony which one of the women and other witnesses later admitted to be false. Their convictions were initially overturned by the U.S. Supreme Court, but the sentences were subsequently reinstated by the Alabama courts after new trials. In the initial appeal, the Supreme Court concluded that Alabama's rush to convict the unrepresented defendants in spite of its own state law requiring the appointment of counsel for indigents constituted a violation of the right to due process under the Fourteenth Amendment.[47] The Scottsboro decision led to the provision of counsel for indigent defendants in death penalty cases. The Supreme Court subsequently expanded the obligation of states to provide defense attorneys for indigent defendants. Attorneys were required in cases involving indigent defendants who were "incapable adequately of making [their] own defense because of ignorance, feeblemindedness, illiteracy, or the like."[48]

The broad application of a constitutional right to counsel within state court systems occurred in the celebrated 1963 case of *Gideon v. Wainwright.* In *Gideon*, the Supreme Court decided that the Due Process Clause of the Fourteenth Amendment required states to provide defense counsel for all indigent defendants facing penalties of six months incarceration or greater.[49] The right to counsel was subsequently recognized for all cases of incarceration in 1972,[50] but was not extended to encompass cases punished merely by fines.[51] Although some states began to provide representation for poor defendants earlier in the twentieth century, it is only in the past few decades that all poor people have been protected by the right to counsel when facing jail or prison sentences.

The Representation of Poor Criminal Defendants

There are three primary methods of providing attorneys for defendants who are too poor to afford to hire their own counsel. In public defender systems, a salaried staff of full- or part-time lawyers provides representation for indigent defendants. The defense attorneys are usually state or local government employees although sometimes private, nonprofit corporations provide public defenders through contracts with local governments. Public defender systems exist in more than 37 percent of counties nationwide and cover a majority of the country's population because of their use in many large cities. Assigned counsels are used in 52 percent of counties. These are private lawyers who are appointed to represent indigent defendants on a case-by-case basis and are then paid by local governments. Alternatively, nearly 11 percent of counties use contract attorneys. In these systems, private attorneys or law firms submit bids to local governments and a contract is awarded for one firm or attorney to provide representation for all poor defendants throughout an entire year for a set contract fee.[52]

A variety of specific problems exist with each defense system, which can detract from the quality of representation received by indigent defendants. The timing of appointment of counsel, for example, can affect case outcomes. Although someone with the means to hire a private attorney may acquire private representation immediately, some jurisdictions do not provide attorneys for indigent defendants until the formal arraignment, which can sometimes be delayed more than thirty days following arrest. By this time the defendant may inadvertently make incriminating statements, witnesses may disappear, and the defense may be placed at a significant disadvantage when pitted against a prosecutor who has been utilizing the government's investigative resources since the day of arrest or earlier. While 39 percent of public defender systems provide counsel to indigent arrestees within twenty-four hours, only 33 percent of assigned counsel and 12 percent of contract systems are appointed as quickly.[53] In addition, the average cost expended per indigent defense case varies widely, from $63 per case in Arkansas to $540 per case in New Jersey. Although these fees reflect, in part, the differences in litigation costs in various regions, the relatively low fees throughout the country raise concerns about the adequacy of attorneys' time devoted to indigents' cases in many jurisdictions.[54]

In public defender systems, attorneys' salaries are relatively low and frequently are lower than those of other government attorneys, including prosecutors. The low salaries can hinder recruitment of outstanding new attorneys, preclude the hiring of experienced trial attorneys, and encourage frequent turnover of personnel. As a consequence, inexperienced and less skilled attorneys may be overrepresented—and potentially overmatched by the prosecution—in some public defender offices. The heavy caseloads assigned to public defenders in some cities may preclude adequate investigation of cases and may restrict opportunities to communicate with clients. Because the number of public defenders in each office is set according to limited budgets, increases in the number of arrests will add to the burden of each defense lawyer and consequently will reduce the resources available for each case. In New York City's public defender program, Legal Aid lawyers have each been responsible for as many as one hundred felony cases simultaneously.[55] Such high caseloads create grave risks that individual defendants will receive inadequate attention and that cases will be delayed for many months while unconvicted, poor defendants remain in jail.

In assigned counsel and contract systems, the attorneys representing indigent defendants may have no genuine knowledge about or interest in criminal law. Unlike the public defenders who have made a commitment to criminal defense work as their current career, assigned counsel may be aspiring corporate or tax lawyers who simply desire additional income. The regular, albeit modest, compensation from the local government may be attractive as dependable income for inexperienced, struggling, and otherwise disinterested lawyers. Moreover, although more than 81 percent of the public-defender counties provide regular training for their attorneys, only 21 percent of the assigned counsel counties and 37 percent of the contract counties provide specialized criminal defense training for lawyers representing indigent defendants.[56]

The modest compensation for assigned counsel and contract attorneys, sometimes as low as $25 per hour with per case maximums of $1,500, are so far below the $10,000 to more than $100,000 that private attorneys would charge for comparable major felonies that indigents' attorneys can have a disincentive for putting forth a devoted effort to each case. In contract systems that use a set fee for all cases in a county during an entire year, the defense attorneys have a strong financial incentive to process cases as quickly as possible (i.e., encourage guilty pleas from their indigent clients) in order to achieve the highest possible profit from the contract at the end of the year. This contract method has been challenged because of its potentially detrimental effect on indigent defendants and at least one state supreme court has found it to be impermissible.[57]

The consequences of being represented by appointed counsel

have been studied by several social scientists. One study of murder charges over two decades found that privately retained attorneys are more successful in securing bail for their clients than are indigents' attorneys, even when severity of charges are controlled.[58] As previously discussed, the inability to secure pretrial release affects not only a loss of freedom, but it also has adverse consequences for retaining jobs, maintaining family relationships, assisting in the preparation of the defense, and receiving a conviction and a sentence. Another study found that bail status and representation by a court-appointed attorney led to a greater probability of receiving a prison sentence even when severity of offense and prior record were controlled.[59] Although a study of three major cities found that there was very little difference in case outcomes received by clients with different types of publicly appointed lawyers, the authors concluded, "Our findings also do not imply that all criminal defendants in these cities are well represented."[60]

Attorney-Client Relationships and Plea Bargaining

The title of one classic study of indigent criminal defendants neatly sums up the attitudes of defendants toward their appointed legal representatives: "Did You Have a Lawyer When You Went to Court? No, I Had a Public Defender."[61] Distrust can develop between attorneys and clients because the defendants perceive their lawyers as representing the government. Because public defenders, assigned counsel, and contract attorneys are all compensated by the same governmental unit which generally also employs the prosecutors and police, the defendants frequently believe that the lawyers have no incentive to put forth a vigorous defense. Indigent defendants presume that because they cannot afford to pay for a lawyer's services, they will automatically be provided with inferior legal representation. Moreover, because the first contact between the attorneys and clients is often in the courtroom moments before a hearing, and the defense lawyers' first words are frequently to the effect that, "If you plead guilty, I can get you a reduced sentence," the defendants perceive that the lawyers are not concerned about their version of the events underlying the alleged criminal violation and are not interested in pursuing an acquittal.

Defendants also observe their attorneys laughing, joking, and communicating in a friendly, familiar manner with the prosecutors who are attempting to have the defendants imprisoned. This can convey the impression that the defense attorneys are really working for the prosecutor rather than for the defendant.[62] The effect of the difficult relationships between appointed counsels and indigent defendants can lead such lawyers to be hostile to their clients, and they may engage in extra strategies to control their clients' attitudes and actions.[63] Although it can be argued that indigent defendants' attitudes about their attorneys are irrelevant to the question of whether poor people suffer detrimental discrimination within the court system, several researchers have questioned such a conclusion:

> Defendants' views of how effective their lawyers are and how well their lawyers treat them are an important index of the extent to which the criminal process in practice honors some of its most fundamental guarantees. And for the defendants themselves, a belief that they are inadequately represented can become a self-fulfilling prophecy if they are not candid with their attorneys, or refuse to accept legal advice, or are so uncooperative that they impair the attorneys' motivation to work effectively for them, the end result may be the same as if the state had failed from the start to provide adequate representation.[64]

In fairness to the work of defense attorneys, it can be said that most defendants misperceive the nature of criminal defense work. Many criminal lawyers, from public defenders to highly paid elite private practitioners, make efforts to develop and maintain good personal relationships with prosecutors. The apparently friendly interaction that disturbs the defendant within the courtroom frequently provides the basis for the development of plea bargain agreements that are beneficial to the defendant. However, the cooperation between the defense attorneys and prosecutors is not simply a function of the defense lawyers' calculated desires to obtain reduced sentences for guilty clients. The defense attorneys' own interests in processing cases quickly encourage cooperative efforts aimed at obtaining guilty pleas.

Defense Attorneys and Guilty Pleas

Abraham Blumberg, a former defense attorney turned social scientist, studied criminal courts and concluded that defense attorneys act as double agents who frequently work to encourage defendants to plead guilty in order to further their own interests in maintaining cooperative relationships in court, speeding case processing, and moving on to new cases.[65] Research on attorneys who actually conduct trials indicates the extent to which cooperation and plea bargaining represent the norm for defense attorneys' behavior. A study in Los Angeles on public defenders who follow clients' wishes by seeking trials rather than facilitating plea bargains has labeled those unusual public defenders as "mavericks."[66]

The incentive for encouraging guilty pleas among indigent defendants may be especially strong for assigned counsel and contract attorneys who not only may lack interest in criminal cases, but who have a strong financial incentive to dispose of cases quickly. Because judges in many jurisdictions are responsible for determining the precise fees paid to assigned counsel, there is an incentive to avoid antagonizing judges by requesting time-consuming trials or by otherwise assuming an adversarial role in representing the indigent client. In addition, because judges sometimes have discretion to appoint assigned counsel, the continuation of income from additional future cases may depend upon maintaining a cooperative relationship with the courtroom workgroup rather than upon zealously representing the defendant. In the double agent role, the defense attorney performs a service for the court system by "cooling out" the defendant, that is, by explaining court procedures in a way that will prepare the defendant and his family to accept the likely outcome of a conviction and sentence. According to Blumberg, even privately retained attorneys act as double agents. Judges frequently cooperate in advancing the attorneys' interests by delaying proceedings so the lawyers can pressure clients to pay delinquent fees or by permitting overly theatrical performances in court so that lawyers can convince clients that they are getting their money's worth.[67] In sum, although courtroom relationships and attorney self-interest may work to the detriment of a wide range of criminal defendants, indigent defendants bear special burdens because of the extra incentives for appointed counsels to cooperate with other court actors regardless of the effects upon the clients' interests.

Trials and Sentencing

Although fewer than 10 percent of criminal cases go to trial, the poor defendants who assert their innocence or demand their right to have a complete trial can face several sources of discrimination in the jury process.

Jury Composition

The jury process is intended to provide citizen involvement in judicial decision making, both to legitimate verdicts and to provide a check upon potential abuses of power by prosecutors and judges. A heterogeneous jury should provide representation from various groups within a community and should presumably ameliorate potential bias based upon race, social status, and other stereotypes. Although there is a common notion that defendants should be tried before a "jury of their peers," the actual composition of juries is usually not completely representative of the various groups within a community. Early in the twentieth century, affluent elites dominated juries when members were drawn from "key men" in the community. The Supreme Court outlawed the practice in 1942,[68] and Congress subsequently required that voters' lists be used as the primary source for jury pools. Although some courts also use drivers' license lists and welfare rolls, the Supreme Court has approved the practice of relying exclusively on voters' lists. In addition, jury pools are sometimes further restricted to voters who take the time to return their juror questionnaires to the clerk of court. According to a comprehensive examination of research on juries, the use of voting lists and questionnaires results in underrepresentation of young people, racial minorities, the poor, and transient people.[69] Citizens in these groups are less likely to be registered as voters and less likely to return questionnaires. As a result, poor defendants may be harmed by biased judgments against them from middle-class and affluent jurors without any countervailing voices on the jury.

In every jury trial, prosecutors and defense lawyers are granted a limited number of peremptory challenges which permit them to exclude a few potential jurors without providing any justification. These challenges are in addition to challenges "for cause" when there is an indication that a juror may be biased in evaluating a particular case. After asking the potential jurors a variety of questions, the attorneys rely on hunches to exclude a few potential jurors that they assume might be more inclined to favor the opposition. Studies indicate that prosecutors disproportionately use these challenges to exclude minorities and young people from juries.[70] The reduced representation from these exclusions can disadvantage poor defendants, who are frequently young or minority group members, by further skewing the jury compositions in favor of middle-class and affluent people.

Because social scientists are not permitted to study decision making in real juries except through the use of post-trial interviews in which jurors frequently alter their descriptions and perceptions of events, jury decision making has frequently been studied in experimental settings. Mock juries, often composed of college students, are confronted with decisions that might face a real jury. Although these experimental situations do not precisely replicate actual jury composition and courtroom situations, they do provide insights into people's biases while performing the role of juror. Results of experimental studies indicate that when simulated jurors are confronted with identical factual situations but with different cues about defendants' socioeconomic status, they are more likely to find poor defendants rather than affluent defendants guilty of criminal offenses based upon the same evidence and same behavior.[71]

Discrimination in Sentencing

Although many states and the federal government have reformed their sentencing procedures to try to insure uniformity in sentences for like offenses by offenders with similar records, the sentences in other states are still left up to the discretion of judges within broad boundaries set by state legislatures. An early review of sentencing studies found evidence of socioeconomic status discrimination in capital punishment cases, but apparent disparities in sentences for other crimes were explained by the greater seriousness of charges and prior convictions for poor defendants.[72] Several subsequent studies have found that poor defendants have a greater likelihood of being convicted and given harsher sentences than more affluent defendants.[73]

The studies do not show direct discrimination against the poor based upon simple prejudices possessed by the judges. Instead, as one researcher noted, there is a "complicated interweaving of extra-legal and legal characteristics."[74] In other words, a variety of factors within the criminal justice system combine in sequence to cause a disproportionate impact upon the poor. Most notably, the inability to make bail and the relative ineffectiveness of court-appointed counsel, two factors which affect poor defendants in particular, have been pinpointed as leading to the discriminatory effects detected in sentencing. As researchers concluded in their study of sentencing for larceny and burglary:

> Our tentative conclusion is that most of the influence of income on the likelihood of imprisonment among defendants studied is explained by the poorer opportunity of the low-income defendant for bail and his greater likelihood of having a court-assigned, rather than a privately retained attorney.[75]

More severe sentences have also been applied to juvenile offenders of lower socioeconomic status.[76] In addition, there is evidence that homicide cases are more vigorously pursued by prosecutors when defendants are unemployed and especially when the victim had a higher occupational status than the suspect.[77] The most important study to question these conclusions has itself become the focus of analyses concerning the difficult issues involved in defining and applying variables for socioeconomic status.[78]

In addition to the problems of bail and court-appointed attorneys, the local legal culture may affect the treatment of poor defendants because of the types of lawyers who are selected to become judges. Martin Levin's study of judges in Pittsburgh and Minneapolis provides the most well-known example. In Pittsburgh, where judges frequently have working-class backgrounds and work their way up through the partisan political organizations within various neighborhoods, the judges' empathy with and understanding of poor defendants lead them to tailor punishments according to the particular needs and circumstances of each individual. As a result, the sentences are less harsh than in Minneapolis, where the appointed, nonpartisan judges are drawn from affluent, elite backgrounds.[79]

The Death Penalty and Poor Defendants

Capital punishment provides a special area of concern for the equal treatment of defendants. The death penalty is the ultimate, irreversible punishment that the government can mete out to criminal offenders. Although social scientists using their best scientific methods have shown that the death penalty is still imposed in an arbitrary and discriminatory manner, the Supreme Court has approved continued imposition of capital punishment. In a significant discrimination case, an unsuccessful challenge to the death penalty utilized an analysis of 230 different factors in hundreds of cases to provide strong evidence of racial discrimination in capital sentencing in Georgia.[80]

Although racial discrimination has received the greatest attention in regard to capital punishment, there is evidence of discrimination against the poor as well. One basis for discrimination is that homicide suspects are convicted of and punished for more serious murder offenses when low-status defendants are accused of killing victims with high occupational status.[81]

Because prosecutors are permitted to seek "death qualified juries" by excluding jurors who are categorically opposed to the imposition of capital punishment, the process of seeking death qualified juries leads to disproportionate exclusion of minority and poor jurors.[82] Simulated homicide trials indicate that poor jurors may perceive events differently in assessing the acceptability of behavior. For example, in order to impose the death penalty, the prosecutor must normally establish that a killing was premeditated. As one study indicates, however, "jurors from lower socioeconomic backgrounds did not find the fact that the defendant was carrying a knife exceptional, and were less likely than middle-class jurors to infer premeditation from this fact."[83] Thus, a crucial element for most capital convictions may be inferred by death qualified, middle-class jurors who attach extra significance to an everyday act by a poor defendant (e.g., carrying a knife) because their experience indicates that knives are only carried for criminal purposes. Studies indicate that jurors in capital cases are more prone to find defendants guilty because juries lack diversity and countervailing viewpoints on crime and punishment.[84] When this conclusion is considered in light of the exclusion of poor people from death qualified juries, there is a great risk of unequal application of death sentences to poor defendants.

A study of Florida murder cases found that defendants are more likely to be indicted, convicted, and sentenced to death if they are represented by court-appointed attorneys rather than by privately retained counsel or public defenders. The detrimental consequences of having appointed counsel obviously have a disproportionate impact upon indigent defendants who are too poor to hire their own attorneys. A major problem contributing to this discriminatory impact in Florida is that court-appointed attorneys are paid a maximum of only $3,500 in capital cases—a sum which does not even approach the $100,000 or more that private attorneys would charge for similar cases. Not surprisingly, inexperienced attorneys are frequently the only lawyers willing to accept such appointments. In a survey of judges who appoint attorneys, judges admitted that they do not appoint the best attorneys for capital cases and one judge even reported that a colleague intentionally appointed inept lawyers to represent defendants charged with particularly heinous crimes.[85] Instead of striving to provide the fairest possible trials, these judges seem to be interested in insuring that defendants are convicted of murder charges.

In 1989, the Supreme Court made its own contribution to the risk of inadequate representation by ruling, 5 to 4, that death row inmates are not entitled to have a court-appointed attorney after the initial appeal of their convictions.[86] Thus, the opportunities for federal appellate courts to identify errors made by trial courts or by court-appointed lawyers have been reduced for poor people convicted of capital offenses. These subsequent reviews had previously resulted in death sentences being set aside because of defects in nearly two-thirds of all cases. Volunteer lawyers are unwilling to fill the need for appellate assistance because volunteers in such cases incurred an average of over $10,000 in uncompensated, out-of-pocket expenses. The reduction of legal protection for poor defendants facing capital punishment is made all the more disturbing because two poor defendants who had been sentenced to die were found to be innocent in 1989 after serving many years in prison.[87] If there are accelerated executions because of reduced opportunities for court review, innocent people may be put to death. Because the risk of discrimination and error is greater in cases of poor defendants who are less likely to make bail and less well represented by appointed counsel, the reduction in opportunities for appeals will have the greatest impact upon the poor.

Appeals and Prisoner Litigation

Indigent prisoners are generally entitled to appointed counsel for their first appeal in a state court. By contrast, when prisoners seek a subsequent appeal or a discretionary appellate review by petitioning an appeals court to hear a case which the court can decline to hear if it so chooses, indigent prisoners are not entitled to an appointed attorney.[88] Prisoners are permitted to file actions *pro se,* namely representing themselves without an attorney, but it is very difficult for uneducated prisoners to present their claims effectively according to required legal procedures. Public interest groups generally only represent prisoners in major class action suits or in the relatively few cases that might affect significant legal precedents.

The risk of ineffective appellate representation is compounded by evidence that appellate courts prefer to devote their time and resources to civil cases presented by lawyers from prestigious firms. A study of California's intermediate appellate court indicated that criminal appeals required a greater showing of legal error in order to garner reversal, suffered the greatest reductions in opinions carefully written for publication, and experienced a high rate of dismissals from screening by court staff before ever being considered by judges.[89] Poor prisoners who lack adequate legal representation face particularly difficult hurdles in attempting to have their cases considered by appellate courts.

Prisoners generally can file three types of actions that may result in appellate review. The first action is usually a direct appeal of their conviction and sentence in a state appellate court based upon asserted errors in the criminal justice process. A second action is the traditional writ of *habeas corpus* which is enshrined in the U.S. Constitution. In *habeas corpus* actions, prisoners can contest the basis for their incarceration and seek a second state court review of alleged errors. If unsuccessful in the state court, they may seek a subsequent review by a federal judge. The third type of action, which is actually a civil case, is a civil rights suit claiming that federal constitutional rights have been violated by governmental actors in the criminal justice system. Because of ineffective grievance procedures within correctional institutions, lawsuits are frequently seen by prisoners as the only means they have to assert complaints about conditions or treatment behind prison walls.

The Supreme Court attempted to insure that poor prisoners have necessary access to the courts by requiring that prisons provide prisoners with legal assistance or a law library.[90] Most correctional institutions have opted to provide libraries, although these libraries frequently do not contain all of the materials necessary for preparing cases. Merely having access to a law library does not insure that prisoners can effectively pursue appeals or file cases regarding perceived violations of their constitutional rights. Significant numbers of prisoners have little formal education, low I.Q.s, or learning disabilities. In addition, many prisoners in some states speak Spanish as their primary language and have little hope of using English language legal materials available in a law library. As one federal judge notes:

> To expect untrained laymen to work with entirely unfamiliar books, whose content they cannot understand, may be worthy of Lewis Carroll, but hardly satisfies the substance of constitutional duty.
>
> Access to full law libraries makes about as much sense as furnishing medical services through books like: "Brain Surgery Self-Taught," or "How To Remove Your Own Appendix," along with scalpels, drills, hemostats, sponges, and sutures.[91]

In addition to the difficulties facing indigent prisoners who attempt to undertake legal research in order to represent themselves, the *pro se* litigants face a significant challenge in attempting to phrase their complaints in accordance with proper legal terminology and required court procedures. Judges and their law clerks must attempt to sort through many handwritten, incomprehensible claims submitted by prisoners in order to determine if there are any valid legal issues that require consideration. Because the judicial officers may have a personal interest in quickly terminating these routine and repetitive cases filed by unsympathetic claimants, there is a risk that prisoners' cases, especially those filed by poor prisoners not represented by attorneys, will be dismissed without receiving adequate consideration.[92]

Although studies of prisoners' cases disagree about whether judges adequately review claims submitted by prisoners, it is well established, for example, that more than 90 percent of prisoners' civil rights cases are dismissed prior to any hearing by a judge.[93] The high rate of summary dismissals is frequently attributed to the prevalence of frivolous complaints filed by prisoners. It is clear, however, that the obstacles facing poor prisoners who attempt to represent themselves in court, including those with legitimate complaints, contribute to their general lack of success in having cases move beyond the initial stage of filing a soon-to-be dismissed complaint.

The Prospects for Reform

The variety, interconnectedness, and cumulative nature of the factors contributing to the discriminatory outcomes experienced by the poor within the criminal justice system make reform both difficult and unlikely. The discretionary decision-making authority vested in police officers, prosecutors, defense lawyers, and judges cannot be readily removed or controlled and therefore the risk of bias remains ever present.

Legislatures have attempted to limit the discretion of judges by mandating specific sentences for various offenses, thus assuring uniformity in punishment. Such reforms have normally been subverted by a variety of factors inherent in the sequential characteristics of the criminal justice system. Police and prosecutors, for example, simply adjust their discretionary decisions at the stages of arrests, setting charges and plea bargaining to ensure that the actors within the criminal justice system continue to control outcomes.

Specific reforms to reduce the discriminatory effects of the bail system have been attempted in several cities, but they frequently fail to achieve acceptance and institutionalization within the criminal justice system.[94] Samuel Walker advocates implementation of speedy trials as one plausible means of reducing the detrimental effects of pretrial detention upon poor defendants.[95] The effectiveness of this reform in reducing disparities in sentencing would be undercut by the continued problems in using court-appointed counsel who do not adequately represent the interests of indigent defendants. This problem can only be improved by devoting more resources to the defense of indigents—a resource allocation policy that will never have any effective political constituency and that is already experiencing erosion through decisions of the Supreme Court.

CHAPTER THREE

The Poor and the
Civil Justice System

C ourts provide a forum for airing private disputes between individuals, groups, and organizations. In civil cases, one party calls upon the judiciary to make a declaration concerning the respective rights of the disputants to property, monetary compensation for injuries, performance of a contract, prohibitions on harmful behavior, or some other asserted entitlement. Most civil cases do not result in judges or juries deciding in favor of one of the disputants, but instead lead to negotiated settlements between the parties. The negotiation process is sometimes guided by the direct involvement of judicial officers, but even without intervention by judges, the settlement discussions are inevitably constrained and influenced by the threat of continued court action with its potential for an uncertain "winner-take-all" outcome. Thus, the processing of civil cases has been characterized as "bargaining in the shadow of the law."[1]

Although civil cases range in complexity from uncontested divorces and small claims cases to complicated, multi-million dollar antitrust actions, such cases can be roughly divided into disputes between private parties and, alternatively, actions aimed at generating social change, such as desegregating a school system or improving conditions at a correctional institution. The two categories of civil cases are distinguishable in theory but, as Joel Grossman and Austin Sarat have noted, "[t]he distinction between remedy-seeking and reform-oriented participation is, in practice, not easy to make."[2] Some cases may be moved from one category to the other by the actions of litigants or judges. Despite the artificial nature of this rough dichotomy, dividing civil cases into these two broad categories is useful for purposes of illuminating the civil justice system's consequences for poor people.

Cases in Civil Court

Obviously, not all disputes between private parties will be brought to court. People and organizations continually feel aggrieved by the actions of others. Experiences which are perceived as harmful, ranging from the annoyance of a neighbor's barking dog to a serious injury caused in an automobile accident, may all potentially result in civil litigation, yet the overwhelming majority of grievances will never reach the court system. Grievances must be transformed into disputes and then shaped in accordance with legal procedures in order to become civil court cases.

The Initiation of Litigation

According to Marc Galanter's well-known characterization of the process underlying the development of civil litigation,[3] only some perceived injuries, namely "grievances," will be voiced to the offending party in the form of "claims." Some people simply "lump it" when they perceive an injury or when the offending party refuses to respond to their claim. People who persist in asserting their claims after the offending party has refused to satisfy their grievances have reached the stage of an active "dispute," some of which will be resolved through negotiation and others of which will be abandoned.

In a study of "middle-range" grievances worth $1,000 or more, out of 1,000 grievances, only 449 became disputes and only 103 led to the next step of consulting a lawyer.[4] Grievances are abandoned for a variety of reasons, including a lack of information about possible avenues for remedies, concern about the costs of pursuing claims, unwillingness to generate conflict, and a perception that official channels for remedies will be unresponsive.[5] These factors are especially powerful hindrances for poor people.

For example, higher income households are much more likely to complain about problems they encounter with the goods they buy than are poor households.[6] Increased assertiveness in pursuing claims is evident among people with higher education levels who presumably are better able to identify remediable grievances, know how to pursue their claims, and have better access to resources for seeking satisfaction. One study indicated that people in poorer communities may resort to confrontational self-help to settle disputes, including the use of retaliatory property damage or even violence.[7] One purpose of law is to prevent the social disorder that flows from self-help justice. The government maintains order through its regulations and interventions designed to clarify rights and enforce entitlements. If poor people lack access to the legal protections which are supposed to be available through judicial processes, then they may be left with the choice of "lumping it" or seeking to remedy grievances themselves.

The Role of Lawyers

Lawyers play an important role in transforming disputes into legal cases. Therefore, obtaining legal assistance is a critical element in initiating civil litigation. Unlike the right to counsel secured for criminal defendants by the Sixth Amendment of the Constitution, there is no comparable right to legal assistance for indigent parties in civil cases. Thus, poorer people are less likely to be able to afford the requisite legal advice required to shape their issues into forms acceptable for presentation in courts and to undertake the complicated processes of filing papers, engaging in the legal "discovery" process for gathering evidence, and completing the other specialized processes in civil litigations. Research indicates that more affluent people generally have better access to legal advice, but some studies have shown that in specific kinds of cases, such as torts and juvenile matters, lower status people are more likely to obtain the assistance of lawyers.[8]

Although some poor people are eligible to receive free or reduced-cost legal assistance from legal services agencies, many others are undoubtedly deterred from pursuing cases in court because of the prohibitive expense of hiring a lawyer. Those poor people who are fortunate enough to receive the services of a private attorney for no fee or reduced rates will frequently not receive the same treatment as more affluent, paying clients. According to one study of attorneys in private practice, "[t]he inclination of the attorneys was, typically, to settle their [no fee/low fee] cases and get back to the important paying business."[9]

In addition to transforming disputes into legal actions, lawyers also serve as gatekeepers whose discretionary judgments determine which disputes will move forward to seek redress within the court system. Without a lawyer willing to carry the case forward into the court, most cases will be effectively filtered away from the judicial system. As Harry Stumpf has noted about the role of lawyers in civil litigation:

> The judicial process is anything but self-activating; parties with disputes must be brought to court. Moreover, the process itself is complex, with a host of rules of substance and procedure with which only the attorney is familiar. In their capacity as experts in these matters, lawyers are given a monopoly in determining who has access to the ju-

dicial system, at what price, under what conditions, and often to what ends.[10]

Lawyers can encourage or discourage people about the prospects for their cases. Moreover, the lawyers' decisions about which cases to pursue in court will be determined not merely by the merits of the claim and the prospects for a successful outcome, but also by the expected financial remuneration for the attorneys' efforts. Some potentially meritorious claims will never be pursued because the anticipated attorneys' fees and litigation costs will outstrip any possible recovery. As one scholar has noted, "[o]ften attorney's fees, running at $50 per hour or more, quickly exceed what a litigant can hope to recover in court."[11] Attorneys' incentives and the organization of legal services within a state can determine which clients receive information, encouragement, and assistance in pursuing cases through the courts. For example, one study in Wisconsin found that information and legal assistance on consumer protections laws were available to affluent people and businesses but not to ordinary consumers.[12]

In the study of 1,000 "middle-range" ($1,000 or more) grievances, out of the 103 disputes that reached attorneys for consideration and advice, only 50 civil cases were actually filed.[13] Because poor people have more limited access to lawyers' services than do businesses and more affluent people, their cases are less likely to be among the relatively few grievances that are transformed into lawsuits.

The Costs of Civil Litigation

The costs of obtaining legal counsel can be substantial. Lawyers are generally paid either according to an hourly rate or on a contingency fee basis in which the attorneys generally receive one-third of the award or settlement. Hourly fees for lawyers' services usually range from $50 per hour to several hundred dollars per hour. Just a few hours of work by an attorney can quickly exceed the resources possessed by people whose incomes are devoted to paying their food, housing, and other bills every month. Lawyers who bill by the hour have a self-interested incentive in maximizing their incomes by billing for as many hours as they can. According to one scholar:

> [T]he lawyer will sell clients legal services, not at the lowest price consistent with modest profits, but at the highest price the client will bear. Furthermore, the lawyer will sell those hours and activities, not at the

least needed to increase the probability of achieving the result the client desires, but at the maximum hours and services the client will authorize.[14]

Obviously, lawyers will have a strong preference to accept cases from affluent people and businesses who can afford to pay for a substantial number of hours on each case.

Poor people may be able to obtain the services of private attorneys on a contingency fee basis if the lawyers believe that there is a sufficient probability of receiving a substantial award or settlement. Thus, poor people can most readily obtain representation in cases of serious personal injuries. The lawyer will have a strong personal interest in winning the case and therefore will invest the law firm's money in covering the costs of litigation. Representation of this sort is not available in other kinds of cases which comprise the bulk of grievances by poor people and others in society. Disputes between neighbors, landlords and tenants, employers and employees, and other private individuals usually do not involve sufficient amounts of money to attract contingency fee representation.

One particular problem with contingency fees is that the lawyers have an incentive to conclude the case as quickly as possible in order to maximize their pay based upon a minimum number of hours of work. Thus lawyers may negotiate early settlements that reduce the potential award that could be obtained by their clients.[15]

Unbeknownst to most lay people, attorneys utilize paralegals, law students, and other staff members. These subordinates often perform many of the civil litigation tasks for which clients are billed at a high hourly rate. Many routine legal matters entail merely filling out forms and filing them with the appropriate court or government agency. For wills, divorces, adoptions, and other matters, lawyers meet with clients but nonlawyer staff members frequently perform the actual work. Costs of litigation could be reduced by permitting paraprofessionals to handle these tasks on their own, but lawyers have used their political strength to prevent any weakening of their monopoly over legal services. Bar associations have even worked to prosecute paralegals who help poor people fill out forms for uncontested divorces and adoptions. As Stumpf has commented:

> It has long been recognized that much of the work of lawyers is routine and could be performed by paraprofessionals, thereby reducing the overall cost of legal advice. Paraprofessionals are indeed growing in number, but it appears their potential for cost reduction has been thwarted by legal offices that employ them at relatively low salaries

but use the resultant savings to increase the salaries of partners in the firm.[16]

Court Costs

In addition to the significant cost of obtaining a lawyer, there are court costs which can prevent poorer people from bringing their disputes to the judiciary. In all courts there are filing fees which must be paid in order to initiate a case. Filing fees can range from $15 for small claims cases to $50 or more in general state court cases. The filing fee for federal cases is $120. Although it is appropriate that users of the court system should bear some of the case-processing costs and that litigants should be willing to put up some money in order to pursue a lawsuit, the fees can discourage poorer people from bringing claims, especially in disputes over relatively small amounts of money. Poor people generally have an opportunity to request a waiver of filing fees if they can prove that they lack resources and income, but approval of the waiver is in the hands of court officials. In addition, people who lack money may own a car or some other property which might preclude recognition of indigent status.

In some cases, filing fees can serve as an absolute bar to poor people who seek to present their claims in court. The Supreme Court has determined that there is no right to waiver of fees for poor people who initiate bankruptcy cases[17] or who seek court review of a reduction in welfare benefits.[18] Thus, as one scholar has concluded, "judicial resolution of [the *Kras* and *Ortwein* cases by the Supreme Court] has created the legal irony that one may be too poor to go bankrupt or to get welfare."[19]

The rules of civil court procedure can place additional costs and other burdens upon litigants. In order to have another party brought into court, a litigant may have to initiate the case in the district in which the defendant lives rather than in the plaintiff's home district. Although this requirement was created for the rational purpose of preventing the use of civil litigation for harassment by dragging a defendant to another jurisdiction, the attendant increased costs can place a greater burden upon claimants who lack the resources to travel or to secure an additional attorney in another city.

Trial Preparation Costs

In addition to filing fees and the expense of hiring attorneys, the process of civil litigation itself is expensive. Lawyers typically spend months and sometimes years involved in the legal investigation process, known as "discovery," in which they obtain documents from the opposing side and record the testimony of potential witnesses. In taking "depositions," sworn testimony from witnesses prior to trial, the litigants have to pay for a court reporter to attend each deposition session and subsequently to create a transcript of the testimony. There are costs expended for attorneys and court reporters to travel to various cities in order to conduct depositions of witnesses located elsewhere. There are also significant fees paid to expert witnesses. According to one judge, "doctors customarily receive from $500 to $1,000 or more for testifying in a simple routine accident case."[20] It can cost even more money if the expert's services are needed for more than one or two days. Corporations have paid economists and other experts tens of thousands of dollars to serve as expert witnesses in complex litigation—sums which are obviously well beyond the means of ordinary individuals, especially poor people.

An excellent description of civil litigation, including its substantial costs, is contained in Gerald Stern's book, *The Buffalo Creek Disaster.*[21] Stern was the lawyer for several hundred poor people in West Virginia who suffered severe consequences when a coal company's dam broke and unleashed a flood that killed more than 125 people and which left hundreds of people homeless. The victims were extremely fortunate that Stern's wealthy Washington, D.C. law firm agreed to accept the case on a contingency fee basis. In the course of the two years of trial preparation prior to the ultimate negotiated settlement, the law firm spent more than $500,000 on litigation costs and invested more than 40,000 person-hours of work on the case. In addition, the law firm could afford to hire the best psychiatrists and psychologists from the faculties of Harvard and Yale to serve as expert witnesses in the case. Although the wealthy law firm was the equal of the coal company in this case, most individuals who battle wealthier people or companies in court will be forced to settle at a relatively early stage because they cannot match their opponents' resources for prolonging litigation.

Lawyers involved in civil litigation know that the party with the most money can frequently prolong any lawsuit and force the other side to agree to a settlement for a smaller amount of money, even if the poorer party might have ultimately prevailed in front of a judge or jury. The slow process of litigation can force poor litigants to accept settlement offers because they need money immediately and they cannot afford to wait several years until a full trial runs its course to provide them with complete compensation for their injuries. The pressures upon poorer litigants are increased because of the tremendous backlogs of civil cases in many courts. New criminal cases will go to the head of the line because of a defendant's constitutional right to a speedy trial, but civil cases will often take years to reach a judge.

Other Costs

There are also psychological costs of civil litigation. As Henry Glick points out:

> For businesses, government, or other organizations that use courts as part of their regular activities, psychological costs probably are not much of a problem, but for individuals who are rarely involved in court cases and who will be personally affected by the proceedings and outcome, the psychological load may be equal to or heavier than the financial one.[22]

These costs include the significant period of time consumed by cases during which claimants do not receive sorely needed money. Anger and distress over the dispute may worsen as time passes and the ultimate outcome seems more uncertain. In addition, people may feel a loss of control over the dispute because many lawyers prefer that their clients remain completely dependent upon them for advice and action in cases. These costs may weigh more heavily upon poorer people who lack both understanding of the judicial process and access to legal resources. The burden may be even greater for less affluent people because they may lack confidence in the fairness of governmental institutions.

Poor people experience an additional overriding cost with especially detrimental consequences. There is a significantly lower rate of success in court for "one-shotters" than for "repeat players." Organizational entities, such as insurance companies, are frequent users of judicial resources which can utilize specific advantages to increase their success in litigation, especially when in disputes with individuals, who typically are unsophisticated litigants. As Marc Galanter has argued in a review of the literature on civil litigation:

> [The repeat player] enjoys a number of advantages in the litigation process. Briefly, these advantages include: ability to structure the transaction; expertise, economies of scale, low start-up costs; informal relations with institutional incumbents; bargaining credibility; ability to adopt optimal strategies; ability to play for rules in both political forums and in litigation itself by litigation strategy and settlement policy; and ability to invest to secure penetration of favorable rules.[23]

The ultimate cost for poor individuals is a reduced ability to succeed in the civil litigation process because they lack resources and other advantages possessed by larger, more affluent, and more experienced litigants.

The Poor in Specific Court Contexts

Small Claims Court

Small claims court processes were developed to encourage quick, informal, and inexpensive resolution of disputes involving modest sums of money. Each state limits which claims can be brought into the small claims process, with maximum amounts ranging from a few hundred to a few thousand dollars. The primary intention of the small claims concept was to create an informal forum in which common people could represent themselves and avoid the expense of acquiring legal counsel. Lawyers serving as referees frequently preside over the proceedings in which each side is supposed to present both its version of the dispute and any documentary evidence relevant to the claim. The hearings tend to be very brief, and decisions are often rendered within days of the hearing.

Small claims processes were developed under the assumption that disputes for modest sums of money were necessarily simple, when in fact such disputes may involve complex issues of evidence and legal principles. Thus, the quick, informal small claims process can oversimplify the nature of disputes and can generate outcomes that do not adequately consider underlying issues. Many cases are heard in less than ten minutes, with few cases lasting as long as twenty minutes.[24]

Rather than create greater access to courts for poor people who lack the resources to enter regular civil litigation, the small claims process is dominated by business interests which use it as an inexpensive method to enforce claims against poor people. A high proportion of plaintiffs in small claims courts are businesses that use the processes to collect debt claims against individuals. As Stumpf has noted, "far from providing a forum for the poor (that is individual, blue- or perhaps white-collar) litigant to afford him his day in court simply and inexpensively, these tribunals have largely become collection agencies for the 'haves' of our society against the 'have nots.' "[25]

Although creditors effectively utilize legal proceedings against poor debtors, poor people do not have equal opportunities to protect themselves through bankruptcy proceedings. The court costs and attorneys' fees required to obtain bankruptcy law protections against creditors prevent poor people from initiating such cases. Instead poor people come into contact with the courts as the targets of legal sanctions sought by more affluent litigants.[26]

Business are frequently represented by attorneys in small claims proceedings, an element which increases their advantage over lay people opposing the debt-enforcement proceedings. In addition, poor people who are summoned to court by creditors have less ability to miss work or arrange for childcare, and these factors contribute to high default rates in small claims cases. Thus businesses can frequently file claims which they automatically win because no one will appear to contest the cases.

In contested cases, court officials pressure the disputants to discuss settling the case prior to conducting a hearing. Although settlement is considered desirable in fostering voluntary resolution of disputes and saving court resources, the unequal bargaining positions between business plaintiffs, particularly those represented by counsel, and individual defendants disadvantages the poorer litigants.

Small claims courts often lack institutionalized mechanisms for enforcing judgments. Thus, prevailing in court may simply lead to additional actions—as well as time and expense—in order for the aggrieved party to receive compensation. Therefore litigants with the resources to pursue additional collection actions possess advantages over one-time users of the small claims process who may easily become disillusioned upon learning that the dispute may remain unresolved after the case has been decided in the court proceeding.

Barbara Yngvesson and Patricia Hennessey have singled out the Harlem Small Claims Court as an outstanding example of a small claims process that avoids many of the problems which plague other courts. The Harlem court is located within the local community and operates at night. It is, therefore, more accessible than daytime courts located at a central, downtown courthouse. The Harlem court uses paraprofessional advocates to assist litigants in court and to publicize the court's availability for helping with dispute resolution. The court possesses legitimacy because it follows standardized procedural rules and draws judges on a rotating basis from the New York City civil court system. Moreover, litigants have the option of submitting cases to arbitration rather than the more formal adjudicatory process. Although Yngvesson and Hennessey also advocate institutionalized mediation procedures and a collection system to enforce judgments, they conclude that the Harlem court's operations demonstrate the possibilities for effective small claims proceedings.[27]

Divorce Proceedings

Because divorce proceedings require a judicial declaration in order to become final, poor people seeking divorces must enter the court system in order to end their marital relationships. As in small claims proceedings, the parties with the greatest access to resources can frequently protect their interests more effectively. A study of negotiated settlements in divorce cases found that financial pressures led the poorer party, usually women, to accept unfavorable settlement terms in order to obtain sorely needed money, even though they might have acquired greater sums if they could afford to wait for the drawn-out adjudication process.[28]

In uncontested divorces, poor people face the prospect of paying attorneys' fees as well as court costs in order to finalize a mutually agreed upon dissolution of marriage. Although a Yale Law School study urged reform of divorce laws to permit people to represent themselves,[29] do-it-yourself divorce kits and lay advisors have been vigorously opposed by lawyers' organizations. In uncontested divorces, lawyers may do no more than instruct their staff members to file standard forms with the court, yet the couple must pay attorneys' fees because bar associations assert that lawyers serve to prevent possible legal complications. Both Stumpf and the authors of the Yale study have argued that lawyers' mandatory involvement in all divorces simply maintains a profitable but unnecessary monopoly for attorneys. As Stumpf says:

> It is difficult to escape the conclusion that the attorney role in divorce action is essentially self-serving. Needed neither for legal or personal counseling reasons in most divorce actions, lawyers nonetheless maintain their monopoly for the pecuniary benefit of a profession gone business. . . . While ever-defended as "in the public interest," the lawyer monopoly over an essentially administrative process is less and less defensible and, in fact, has been shown actually to impede the divorce process.[30]

Alternatives to Formal Litigation

Dissatisfaction with the personal expense, limited court resources, and long delays endemic in formal court procedures has led to a search for alternative methods of addressing disputes. As with small claims courts, which are one type of alternative forum, the goal has been to make dispute processing quicker, less expensive, and more accessible. For example, several cities have created Neighborhood Justice Centers which are designed to process disputes informally and inexpensively through the use of mediators drawn from the community. Thus, disputes can be resolved according to shared community values and within an accessible, informal environment. The centers are designed to handle disputes that might otherwise have been either criminal or civil cases in the formal court system. As Roman Tomasic notes in his critique of the innovation's underlying assumptions, the centers serve as a mechanism for cases to be filtered out of the court system rather than as an alternative forum which attracted disputants voluntarily. Cases involving people are likely to be pushed out of the court system and into the centers. According to Tomasic:

> The U.S. Solicitor General . . . said . . . Neighborhood Justice Centers have the potential of cutting off access to the court system to the poor, an "underclass" that looks to the courts as its only hope. The fact that most complainants in Neighborhood Justice Centers seem to be poor, females, and blacks seems to provide support for this fear.[31]

Richard Abel argues that an expansion of informal mechanisms for handling disputes, although ostensibly intended to improve dispute processing, actually expands state control of disputes while disguising the existence of coercive mechanisms which pressure people to surrender their claims. Paraprofessional state employees, whether called mediators, arbitrators, or small claims referees, replace citizen jurors as the final arbiters of case outcomes. The mechanisms work to neutralize conflict by forcing people to compromise their claims when justice might be better served by vindicating claims and thereby providing aggrieved parties with complete compensation for their losses.[32] As Christine Harrington has observed, "substantive demands for social justice have been overshadowed by experimentation with techniques of alternative dispute resolution."[33]

Reform in the Federal Courts

Several federal district courts have implemented alternative dispute resolution (ADR) processes in an effort to encourage voluntary settlement of civil cases. The ADR techniques include mediation, in which a panel of attorneys places a suggested settlement value on each case; arbitration, in which an attorney serves as a judge in issuing a nonbinding decision; and summary jury trials, in which a real jury of citizens hears evidence during an abbreviated, one-day trial and issues a nonbinding verdict that educates attorneys about their prospects for prevailing in an actual trial.[34]

These mechanisms are credited with successfully encouraging

parties to settle their cases without absorbing federal judges' scarce time and resources for conducting full civil trials. However, the goal of generating settlements is separate from the goal of addressing litigants' claims within disputes. Because participation in ADR procedures is mandatory when ordered by a judge, these mechanisms can serve to prolong litigation and thereby increase court costs and attorneys' fees for litigants seeking vindication through a judicial decision. These nonbinding procedures increase the risk that wealthier litigants can further prolong litigation and thereby place extra pressure on less affluent litigants to settle claims for less money than they might have been awarded at trial. Although relatively few poor people are involved in federal litigation, except for prisoners' cases and Social Security disability appeals, these ADR methods illustrate the extra advantages for more affluent litigants that can be generated through well-intentioned court reforms designed to quicken the pace of dispute processing.

Other court reforms also engender risks of detrimental impacts upon the poor. When Congress gave United States magistrates, a lower tier of judicial officers who assist district judges, the authority to preside over complete civil cases with the consent of litigants, concerns were raised about the possibility of creating a two-track system of justice—district judges for wealthy litigants and magistrates for poor litigants. The reform was intended to increase the federal judiciary's ability to handle civil cases because trials can often be scheduled more quickly if supervised by magistrates rather than by busy district judges. Magistrates, however, do not enjoy the protections of life tenure granted to regular federal judges under Article III of the Constitution. Thus, there are concerns that magistrates might avoid making controversial decisions in order to protect their jobs by gaining renewal of their eight-year terms in office. As a result, if poorer litigants had their cases heard before magistrates, they might not receive the benefit of independent judicial decisions.

One member of Congress questioned whether people would feel pressured to consent to have their cases heard before magistrates:

> It is unlikely that a litigant will hold out for an Article III judge when he or she is poor . . . or is suing for badly needed money and is told by an attorney that with a magistrate the trial will be scheduled sooner and conducted more expeditiously. In cases where a lawyer is not required, it is even less likely that party could resist the lure of speed and economy.[35]

Although there is no clear evidence that the innovation works specifically to harm the interests of poorer litigants, one study indicates that district judges use the consent trial procedure in order to coerce participants in uninteresting or undesirable cases to transfer their disputes to a magistrate.[36] Such pressures are likely to weigh heavily on poorer people because of factors which make affluent litigants' cases more attractive to judges. As one state judge has described judges' preferences in cases:

> Judges also like [cases involving large sums of money and wealthy litigants], for the lawyers are competent, courteous, and well prepared. The judge has an opportunity to research some obscure points of law, to weave his way through precedent, and perhaps to be a bit innovative. No extraneous emotions such as compassion or outrage sully the pure legal doctrines involved. It is no wonder that commercial, corporate, and probate law are the favorites of the legal profession and receive so much of its tender, loving, lengthy, and costly care.[37]

Private Attorneys and Pro Bono Cases

The American Bar Association's (ABA) Model Rules of Professional Conduct declare that lawyers should ensure that poor people have access to adequate legal representation. There is an expectation that lawyers will accept some cases from poor people without charging a fee because of attorneys' ethical obligation to do legal work *pro bono publico*, namely for the benefit of the public good. Model Rule 6.1 states:

> A lawyer should render public interest legal service. A lawyer may discharge this responsibility by providing professional services at no fee or a reduced fee to persons of limited means or to public service or charitable groups or organizations, by service in activities for improving law, the legal system or the legal profession, by financial support for organizations that provide services to persons of limited means.

The rule is not binding and enforceable on lawyers unless it is adopted by their state's legislature or supreme court. Many states had adopted provisions of the ABA's earlier Model Code of Professional Responsibility, but that code contained only ethical exhortations rather than a rule regarding public service.

Because lawyers portray themselves to the public as professionals providing essential services for the good of society, there have long been efforts to encourage or even require lawyers to provide services to poor people without compensation. For example, an advisory committee has urged that New York lawyers be required to devote at least twenty hours each year to public service.[38] A former president of the ABA said, "Our profession will not have met its obligation fully until every lawyer is participating in some way in these (pro bono program) efforts."[39]

Pro Bono in Practice

The expectation that lawyers, as professionals, will provide uncompensated service to the public clashes, however, with the reality that most private attorneys and their law firms function as private businesses devoted to maximizing their profits by attracting and serving clients who can afford to pay substantial legal fees. Any amount of time that lawyers give to poor people is time that cannot be used to gain revenues from paying clients. One study indicates that this clash between business goals and professional ethics leads lawyers to apply highly inconsistent criteria when considering whether to accept a pro bono case.[40]

Many lawyers object to the notion that they should be forced to give their professional services away. Lawyers and their organizations are deeply divided over the issue of whether lawyers should be required to serve the poor, and the Supreme Court is divided on the issue as well. In a split decision in 1989, mixing unusual coalitions of liberal and conservative justices on both sides of the issue, the Supreme Court ruled that a statute passed by Congress cannot be utilized by judges to require attorneys to undertake uncompensated representation of poor clients.[41]

Studies of lawyers' pro bono work indicate the limited extent to which attorneys donate time to the poor, as well as the differential treatment that less affluent clients receive. One study found that lawyers provide only a modest level of service to the less affluent. About 60 percent of the lawyers responding to a survey indicated that they spend less than 5 percent of their billable hours doing pro bono work and almost half of them spent no time at all. In addition, many of these cases which lawyers considered pro bono were really clients who failed to pay after services were performed rather than instances of attorneys altruistically donating their time to poor people. In pro bono work outside of normal working hours, most of the donated time provided services for church and community groups or for family and friends of the lawyer. In sum, there is relatively little pro bono work provided for poor individuals and their legal problems.[42]

In *The Buffalo Creek Disaster*, the Washington, D.C. lawyers initially represented the poor flood victims because the firm permitted one lawyer each year to devote time to pro bono cases. The firm deserved praise for spending several hundred thousand dollars in vigorously pursuing the lawsuit against the coal company. Although the case began as a pro bono effort and ultimately achieved a substantial settlement for the victims, the law firm received a handsome profit from its efforts. Their $3 million contingency fee went well beyond the expenses they had incurred and even exceeded the $2 million received for the mental suffering of 226 children who lost loved ones and homes in the disaster.[43] As with the lawyers who label their work pro bono after the fact simply because a client fails to pay, the *Buffalo Creek* example demonstrates that the actual level of services intentionally donated to poor people can be overestimated by relying upon lawyers' varying definitions of what constitutes "work for the benefit of the public."

One study found that lawyers worked harder for their paying clients. They quickly agreed to settlements in the cases of poor clients in order to devote their time and energy to paying clients. In addition, a primary motivation for doing pro bono work was not to provide services for the poor, but to cultivate clients who might subsequently hire the lawyer. Lawyers hoped that the clients' financial circumstances might change in the future, that the case might generate favorable publicity, or that the client might steer friends and relatives to the attorney for paid cases. Although this evident self-interest might be perceived as a positive factor which would encourage lawyers to provide greater assistance to poor people, in fact most pro bono work was actually supplied to middle-class people whose immediate circumstances prevented them from paying for legal services. The study indicated that pro bono work is not provided to the neediest sectors of society because the truly poor lack necessary connections with the intermediaries, such as doctors, ministers, and coworkers, who frequently persuade lawyer-acquaintances to accept cases for middle-class people.[44]

During the 1970s and 1980s, some law firms began to reduce their pro bono legal work. Rising overhead costs and increased competition between law firms led to greater limitations on lawyers donating time to non-paying clients. Furthermore, law firms moved to limit their attorneys' contributions to complex cases because they preferred that their lawyers volunteer for pro bono cases capable of being completed very quickly. Despite the diminished services for the poor by law firms, many individual attorneys and bar associations have increased their contributions to pro bono work.[45]

Legal Services Agencies

Attempts to create organizations to serve the poor's legal needs in civil matters began with the German Legal Aid Society in New York City in the 1870s. Through the first half of the twentieth century, although agencies were created in several dozen cities to provide legal services to the poor, most cities had no civil legal aid organizations. The agencies that did exist tended to struggle with tiny budgets supported primarily by private donations.

In the 1960s, as part of President Johnson's "War on Poverty," the federal government created neighborhood legal services offices throughout the country to provide civil legal aid to indigent people. The agency, which began as a unit of the Office of Economic Opportunity, eventually became a completely separate government agency with its own governing board called the Legal Services Corporation. People who meet requirements for low incomes and who have few assets are eligible to seek legal help from Legal Services offices. Because legal services programs are not high priorities for government and are not forcefully supported by powerful political interests, such programs lack the resources necessary to fulfill the continuing need for legal counseling and representation for low-income people.

Legal Services and Social Reform Litigation

Legal services programs came under attack from local political and economic interests when attorneys began to file broader legal actions contesting governmental policies that adversely affected poor people.[46] The strongest attack on legal services came from then-Governor Ronald Reagan of California, who was upset when suits by legal services lawyers prevented him from dropping 160,000 poor people from a medical assistance program, forced farm owners to pay a minimum hourly wage to agricultural workers, and invalidated an English language literacy requirement for voting. The Nixon administration assisted the attack upon legal services by moving administrative authority from the national director to regional program directors who were more susceptible to local political pressures.[47] According to one study, this decentralization has effectively limited litigation aimed at reforming societal institutions:

> Especially in a program like legal services for the poor, which at the national level operates constantly under conditions of budgetary uncertainty, local programs are vulnerable to efforts by powerful local groups to set priorities and define appropriate activity. Consequently, in many communities local organizations effectively encourage service to individual clients and constrain social reform activity.[48]

Political pressure to limit legal services lawyers' activities on behalf of the poor reached a peak during the Reagan presidency.

Reagan initially proposed abolishing legal services programs and advocated returning responsibility for helping the poor to private attorneys. Because Congress resisted presidential efforts to abolish the agency, the Reagan administration adopted the alternative approach of cutting the agency's budget every year and appointing as directors of the Legal Services Corporation people who were opposed to the existence of the program. These directors attempted to channel funds to outside legal organizations which were pursuing right-wing political causes.

As Jerome Corsi has noted, the efforts of the Reagan administration to transfer legal aid responsibilities to the private sector reflect either ignorance or apathy about the history of legal services for the poor. According to Corsi, "[t]he neglect of the poor by the private bar has been a primary impetus behind legal aid movements throughout this century."[49] The conclusions of one researcher who studied legal-services programs indicate that private attorneys cannot be expected to serve the needs of the poor adequately. Private attorneys lack specialized knowledge of issues affecting low-income people. They have no financial or political incentive to pursue cases vigorously, especially those cases that might threaten established political or economic interests. In fact, because of the frequent connections between lawyers and business interests within communities, attorneys may be reluctant to pursue tenant complaints against landlords or consumer claims against businesses and banks. In addition, community pressures can deter lawyers from representing poor people in controversial cases, such as medical malpractice and civil rights.[50]

Litigation for the Vindication of Rights and Legal Reform

Reform-oriented litigation is initiated by public-interest organizations which carefully select the cases to pursue. Because of limited resources, they generally can undertake only a few cases aimed at altering governmental policies. A study of public-interest legal organizations revealed that their resources were increasingly absorbed by fundraising activities and that they had experienced greater opposition from federal judges and governmental agencies during the Reagan administration.[51] Court victories in reform litigation often have little practical effect because of the obstacles to successfully implementing judicial orders. Research on the implementation of court decrees has shown that institutions have tremendous ability to resist, distort, and even ignore judges' orders for years following a case decision.[52] In addition, opponents of reform can prolong disputes through appeals and further litigation.

Although the critics of legal services programs have been most disturbed by court victories asserting the rights of the poor against government and organized interests, litigation on behalf of the poor has merely reformed some institutions instead of attacking harmful inequalities in society. Some commentators see possibilities for legal processes and decisions to encourage social change, because opportunities for litigation can help to win symbolic victories which mobilize political action and aspirations.[53] But, as Jack Katz has argued, "[t]he thrust of litigation against [exploitation of the poor] is not to eliminate poverty but to civilize it."[54] Litigation against government has sought to provide clearer definition and protection of separate programs designed to benefit the poor specifically. A minority of reform-seeking suits seek to integrate poor people into other sectors of society; most cases seek to obtain entitlements for the poor as a segregated segment of society. Katz concluded from his study of legal services:

> [O]verall, poverty reform litigation on the one hand attacks exclusions of the poor from the private job market and distinctive methods for exercising economic power over the poor in consumer transactions; and on the other hand, it spurs public agencies which specialize in a clientele of poor people to activate recruitment, speed the processing of applications, and discard moralistic in favor of economic criteria for defining beneficiaries. The thrust seems to be to incorporate "poverty," as a distinctive set of behaviors, into the state, where it can be systematically examined and rationally governed by professionals.[55]

Conclusion

The resources required to initiate and sustain civil litigation prevent poor people from fully utilizing the judicial branch of government as a forum for dispute processing. Efforts to provide legal representation for the poor have been limited and incomplete. Because of the political attacks upon the Legal Services Corporation, the services available for handling poor people's legal problems are diminishing even as law schools produce an ever-increasing supply of lawyers who provide legal resources for other sectors of society. As with other political resources used to influence governing institutions, civil litigation remains primarily accessible only to affluent and organized interests.

CHAPTER FOUR

The Poor and Administrative Law

M any of the programs and functions of government are adminis-tered through executive branch agencies responsible for spe-cific policy areas. In the federal government, for example, cabinet-level "secretaries" oversee individual departments, such as the Department of Transportation and the Department of Education, each of which con-tains smaller divisions and individual agencies. There are also indepen-dent agencies, such as the Federal Trade Commission, which exercise quasi-independent authority under the direction of commissioners ap-pointed by the president. These myriad agencies, often collectively la-beled "the Bureaucracy," determine rules and regulations for the alloca-tion of governmental benefits through their delegated authority from Congress and the president. In a democratic system of government, the operations of these agencies in which discretionary decisions are made by invisible "bureaucrats" raise continual questions about the ability of elected officials and the public to maintain accountability and supervi-sion over complex, powerful organizations.

Judicial Process and Administrative Agencies

Poor people and the judicial process come into contact with adminis-trative agencies through two primary means. First, poor people may pursue legal challenges to agency policies that arguably violate con-stitutional or statutory provisions. In such cases, as chapters 5 and 6 will discuss more completely in regard to judicial policy making, courts can be insensitive to discriminatory policies. This insensitiv-ity is evident, in part, because the poor are not regarded as a discrete group of people eligible for protection under the Equal Protection Clause of the U.S. Constitution.

There are many examples of poor people challenging the poli-cies of administrative agencies. Although these challenges are occasionally successful, many are rejected because courts are unwilling to recognize harms suffered by less affluent people or because judges defer to agency decisions. For example, in a 1976 case, *Simon v. Eastern Kentucky Welfare Rights Organization*, the Supreme Court rejected a suit challenging Internal Revenue Service rulings granting favorable tax treatments to hospitals which limited provision of medical services to indigent patients.[1] The Court declared that the individual plaintiffs and their welfare rights organization had not demonstrated sufficient interest or injury from the challenged regulation to permit an action against the IRS. In a 1988 challenge to a Department of Agriculture policy that prevented families involved in labor strikes from becoming eligible for food stamps, a divided Supreme Court found the policy to be "rational," and hence legitimate, despite its adverse effects upon the strikers' families.[2] The Court majority ruled that the policy was consistent with government neutrality in labor disputes. The dissenters, however, noted that government policies did not remove tax benefits and other assistance from companies during strikes and therefore these policies singled out and penalized the less affluent striking laborers' families, including children who bore no responsibility for the industrial dispute.

The second contact between the poor and administrative agencies, which is the subject of this chapter, concerns the adjudicative functions of these agencies. When people are challenging an individual decision by an agency rather than an entire policy, they appeal to the adjudicative officers within the agency. For example, if people apply for and are denied welfare benefits, their first appeals are through adjudicative agency processes which frequently contain elements similar to the judicial process in courts but without the same rights, procedural rules, and formalities. According to some scholars, "[i]n recent years, administrative law has seen what has been termed a 'due process explosion.' With increasing frequency, individuals who once meekly accepted adverse actions of administrative agencies are demanding and receiving hearings on their complaints."[3] Depending upon the particular agency's procedures, these "hearings" may range from informal meetings with supervisory personnel to formal, quasijudicial proceedings before an administrative law judge—a judge within an agency whose sole function is to consider and to decide appeals which challenge specific agency decisions.

Rights of the Poor in Administrative Proceedings

The landmark case establishing procedural rights for poor citizens in administrative hearings was *Goldberg v. Kelly*,[4] a case in which the Supreme Court declared that states must provide welfare recipients with a hearing *prior to* terminating benefits. The criteria enunciated by Justice Brennan in *Goldberg* for fair benefit-termination hearings were tailored to fit the needs and abilities of welfare recipients. For example, instead of requiring written submissions, which would demand a significant level of literacy and education for effective preparation, Brennan said that arguments and evidence could be presented orally by the threatened recipient. James Calvi and Susan Coleman identified ten "ingredients" outlined in *Goldberg* to meet the standards of due process for administrative hearings.[5]

1. adequate and timely notice
2. right to confront adverse witnesses
3. right to cross-examine adverse witnesses
4. right to present arguments orally
5. right to present evidence orally
6. disclosure of opposing evidence
7. right to retain an attorney
8. right to an impartial decision maker
9. determination on the record
10. explanation of the decision

Although the *Goldberg* decision appears to establish mandatory standards for fair administrative proceedings, these elements are not present in many administrative proceedings. Because *Goldberg* was directed at welfare termination hearings, agencies may not feel obligated to incorporate these procedures into other kinds of hearings. Moreover, the implementation problems that accompany any judicial decision limit the universal application of judges' declarations. As explained by Calvi and Coleman:

> [A]n administrative agency may continue on its merry way, adjudicating disputes as it has always done, totally oblivious to Supreme Court rulings. Even though *Goldberg v. Kelly* serves as a precedent for future cases, if an agency's procedures go unchallenged, the agency may never have to adopt the *Goldberg* ingredients for its own procedures. This situation serves to remind us that the law is an evolutionary process that sometimes proceeds at an excruciatingly slow pace.[6]

These implementation problems may have significant detrimental effects on poor people who lack the knowledge and resources to identify and challenge inadequate administrative procedures.

The Supreme Court undercut *Goldberg*'s broad message about

procedural rights through subsequent decisions limiting the rights of benefit recipients in other contexts. In *Mathews v. Eldridge*, the Court determined that hearings were not required prior to termination of Social Security disability benefits.[7] The Court majority, containing Nixon appointees who had not participated in *Goldberg*, claimed that there was less need for hearings because disability benefit recipients could subsequently apply for financial assistance from other programs. In dissent, Justices Brennan and Marshall criticized the majority's naive faith in the availability of other programs by noting that the Eldridge family suffered serious deprivations after their disability benefits were terminated without an opportunity for a hearing: "[B]ecause disability benefits were terminated[,] there was a foreclosure upon the Eldridge home and the family's furniture was repossessed, forcing Eldridge, his wife, and their children to sleep in one bed."[8]

The Court also decided in *Ortwein v. Schwab* that indigent people can be precluded from filing for judicial review of state welfare agency decisions if the recipients cannot afford the court filing fee.[9] Thus agency administrative proceedings that do not fulfill expected standards for fair procedures can be immunized from scrutiny if the claimant is too poor to initiate an action in court.

Ernest Gellhorn and Barry Boyer, leading legal scholars on administrative law, have noted the Supreme Court's movement away from providing procedural rights for individuals involved in administrative agency hearings:

> [T]he overall trend is clear: after the initial expansion of procedural rights ushered in by *Goldberg*, the Court has become markedly more reluctant to find that agency action has infringed a constitutionally protected interest, and also more skeptical about the value of trial-type [administrative] procedures.[10]

The reasoning in *Mathews v. Eldridge* indicated that a cost/benefit analysis should be applied to determine what kinds of hearings are necessary in administrative adjudications. For example, can the agency's purposes be accomplished fairly without the administrative burdens and societal costs associated with requiring full evidentiary hearings upon demand? Some commentators have raised questions about the appropriateness of this analysis because a "utilitarian focus on procedural costs and benefits often ignores society's interest in preserving the dignity of the individual and preventing unequal treatment of persons similarly situated."[11] In essence, the Supreme Court's retreat from guaranteeing procedural rights in administrative hearings creates risks that individuals' interests will not be adequately protected in such proceedings.

Case Study: Social Security Disability Benefit Hearings

The Social Security program provides income assistance to qualified people who are unable to work because of a disability. Studies indicate that poor people are more likely to be disabled than are educated, affluent people.[12] Only persons who have worked long enough and have made sufficient contributions to the Social Security system are eligible for the disability benefits. In March 1984, the average monthly benefit was only $455.69 for the 2.5 million beneficiaries.[13] The payments are intended to provide financial assistance for people who cannot support themselves. The benefits are not generous enough to provide a comfortable living for a family. Some studies have indicated that half of all disability recipients are considered poor under government criteria for poverty.[14] Other recipients who rely substantially upon disability payments to support their families could certainly be considered poor even if they do not fall under the government's poverty line.

The Social Security disability adjudicative process represents the largest quasi-judicial system within the federal government. The 800 Administrative Law Judges (ALJ) in the Social Security Administration (SSA) comprise over 60 percent of the total ALJs in the thirty government agencies with adjudicative functions.[15] The Social Security ALJs alone outnumber all of the judges in the federal judiciary. Thus, the Social Security disability program represents an important example of an administrative adjudication process that touches the lives of thousands of less affluent workers who apply for benefits.

The Hearing Process

There is a four-stage process for determining eligibility for disability benefits.[16] Initial applications are filed with local SSA offices which determine if the applicant has made sufficient qualifying contributions to the Social Security program. The local offices then forward the claims to state Disability Determination Service (DDS) offices. The DDS uses a physician and an adjudicator to evaluate the applicant's medical records to determine the severity of impairment. The level of disability is then considered in light of three other factors—the applicant's age, work experience, and education—to determine whether the applicant is unable to work. Decisions are guided by the SSA's tables or grids that indicate which combinations of the four factors will lead to benefit eligibility. In the early 1980s, although the precise rates varied from state to state, an average of 60 percent of all claims were denied after review at the initial state level.[17]

A claimant has the opportunity to appeal the denial of benefits within sixty days. The reconsideration, which is undertaken by the state DDS using the same application and medical records, seldom leads to any different determinations.

A claimant may then request a hearing before an Administrative Law Judge within the Social Security Administration. The ALJ provides a complete reconsideration of all arguments and evidence. Although there are significant questions about the independence of adjudicative officials who do not possess the constitutional tenure and salary protections provided to federal judges, the merit selection process for selecting ALJs has arguably assisted in recruiting competent, independent-minded lawyers for these positions.[18] This hearing provides the first opportunity for a claimant to present his arguments and evidence in person. Claimants may be represented at the hearings by attorneys or lay advocates, or they may represent themselves. Although testimony is taken under oath, the hearing is designed to be informal and nonadversarial. The proceedings are not governed by the usual strict evidentiary rules enforced in court cases. The essence of the hearing, according to Donna Price Cofer, is for the ALJ to "develop the case record on behalf of the SSA (and the American taxpayers) and the claimant, and then make a decision of either total disability or no legally recognized disability."[19] In the early 1980s, ALJs awarded benefits in over 50 percent of the cases they heard.[20]

Adverse ALJ decisions may be appealed to the Social Security Appeals Council within sixty days. Although the Appeals Council may accept new evidence, because it is primarily responsible for simply ensuring that an ALJ's determination conforms with legal and procedural rules rather than rehearing the entire case, the Council reverses very few decisions.

After claimants unsuccessfully exhaust the four administrative stages, they may seek judicial review in the federal courts. District judges and U.S. magistrates who handle such cases for the federal courts do not rehear entire cases but merely review the records to determine if there is substantial evidence to support the ALJ's decision and if the appropriate law and procedures were applied in each case. Federal judicial officers may order hearings in such cases but usually do not. Adverse decisions may be appealed to a circuit court of appeals, but the limited scope of judicial review normally does not lead to many successful appeals. In the twenty-one cases that had been accepted for subsequent review by the U.S. Supreme Court through 1987, the Court demonstrated consistent deference to the decisions of the Social Security Administration.[21]

Important Elements of the Hearing Process

A study of the Social Security hearing process concluded that "many claimants are poorly educated, confused, and uneasy about the process with which they have to deal. There is no doubt, therefore, that claimants require substantial assistance in the development and presentation of their claims."[22] Not surprisingly, there is evidence that claimants are more successful when represented by attorneys.[23] Because contingency fees of up to 25 percent of past due benefits can be awarded directly to attorneys by the SSA, poor claimants should be able to obtain counsel *if* they are aware of that option. However, according to one study, ALJs often fail to inform claimants of their options in regard to securing the services of an attorney:

> In particular, when the claimant indicates, as he often does, that he is unable to pay for a lawyer, the ALJs vary in their response. Often no explanation is given as to the availability of free legal service or the possibility of retaining a lawyer on a contingent fee without paying any retainer.[24]

Although Social Security regulations require the SSA to approve all fees, the adequacy of the agency's efforts to protect claimants from exploitation by attorneys or lay representatives is questionable. According to one study, for any fee below $1500, the 25 percent figure for contingency fees appears to have become presumptively reasonable because nearly 84 percent of fee petitions were granted for the amount requested.[25] The contingency fee may be excessive in some cases because, as one author has noted, an experienced advocate can prepare a case in only about four hours.[26] There is no necessary relationship between the 25 percent contingency fee and the amount of work required for a particular case. By regarding such fees as presumptively reasonable, the SSA may permit attorneys to be overpaid at the expense of disabled workers. Cases vary in difficulty, but the SSA does not appear to scrutinize the efforts of counsel in each case before determining an appropriate fee.[27] As a result, disabled claimants may lose unnecessarily large portions of their relatively modest past due benefits.

As with any other adjudicative process, the disability hearing process is lengthy, especially when considered from the perspective of disabled people who need financial assistance to support their families because they are unable to work. The initial state-level decision takes an average of forty-five days after filing a claim. It usually takes an additional two hundred days to obtain a decision from an ALJ and more than one hundred additional days for a decision from the Appeals Council. In sum, it takes an average of three hundred and fifty days, almost one year, to exhaust all four administrative levels of adjudication.[28] Obviously, subsequent judicial review in the federal courts requires even more time. The existence of these delays and the various stages of appeals may discourage some claimants, especially if they are not represented throughout the process.

The use of prepared tables or grids to determine employability based upon assessments of severity of impairment, age, education, and work experience may detract from accurate, individualized assessments. As one commentator has noted, "the question can also be raised as to whether or not all germane factors can be programmed into the grids and whether or not the grids allow for individual peculiarities."[29] An ALJ interviewed for one study stated that he used the grids because he was legally obligated to apply them. He felt, however, that the grids interfered with his judicial independence and his ability to evaluate accurately each individual claimant.[30] For example, a claimant might accurately assert that he possesses a high school diploma in defining his educational level. Despite his possession of a diploma, however, he may not be able to read well or to do simple arithmetic depending upon the quality of his education. Thus, the simple classification of workers as high school graduates used in the SSA grid may obscure the actual level of education and employability.

Independence of Administrative Law Judges

Under the Administrative Procedure Act which guides agency adjudication in the federal government, claimants are entitled to hearings before impartial officials who are not under the direct control of an executive branch agency. In order to ensure independent decision making, ALJs may be removed from office or disciplined only for good cause. As one leading scholar on the SSA hearing process has noted:

> Given that SSA hearings are non-adversary and that the hearing officer has the responsibility to ensure that the record is complete, the independence of the ALJ is an even more significant factor in this environment than it would be elsewhere.[31]

Although the ALJs are selected through a merit selection process and must have seven years of trial experience, including two years of experience with administrative law, there are significant questions about their ability to make independent, considered judgments on each individual case. Because of the high volume of similar cases, there is a risk that decision making by ALJs may become routinized. This risk may be exacerbated by the use of legal assistants, legal processing clerks, and staff attorneys to assist the ALJs. For example, a staff attorney may be assigned to draft the ALJ's opinion. Such duties necessarily involve discretionary decisions in evaluating and characterizing evidence. Some ALJs use hearing assistants to screen the available data in order to identify only the relevant evidence. In both instances there are risks that by being screened and characterized through the discretionary decisions of subordinates, information relevant to a decision may not receive the full consideration of the ALJ. Thus the adjudicative process can assume "bureaucratic" characteristics as the ultimate decision maker's access to information is both limited and shaped by the actions of subordinates.

A more significant issue derives from the control that the SSA wields over the ostensibly independent ALJs. The SSA, as a component of an executive branch agency under the president and a cabinet officer, has an interest in minimizing the number of approved claims in order to limit budgetary expenditures. Because of the agency's ability to pressure ALJs, the agency's interests may influence the independence of ALJs' decisions and hence deny benefits to deserving claimants.

The SSA may influence ALJs through two primary means. First, the SSA can issue guidelines, regulations, and opinions which limit the ALJs' exercise of discretion. These guidelines and regulations can be formulated to advance the agency's interests. Second, the agency manages adjudicatory activities by determining the location of ALJs, their support staff resources, and other significant elements affecting the work of ALJs. These influences are felt by the ALJs. According to the author of one study:

> ALJs whom we interviewed complained often about pressure to produce . . . and intimated that they feared retaliation in the form of lack of cooperation on requests for reassignment or for new or upgraded staff positions when ALJs failed to respond to these pressures. . . . They complained bitterly about the statistical information compiled concerning ALJ production and reversal rates.[32]

The SSA has indeed exerted pressures upon ALJs not only to produce a certain number of decisions each month but also to make sure that they do not approve too many disability claims. For example, affidavits in a lawsuit filed by five ALJs against the SSA in 1978 indicate that the ALJs were told that if they failed to reduce the number of awards made to claimants, the agency would seek their dismissal from office.[33] Obviously such bureaucratic pressures operate to deter the application of independent, considered judgments in each case, and thereby potentially intimidate ALJs into denying benefits to worthy claimants. ALJs with low productivity rates have faced similar sanctioning pressures and ALJs' productivity rates have been used for determining privileges, such as requested transfers and training at the National Judicial College.[34] Any pressure to increase productivity carries attendant risks that efficiency will be achieved at the expense of thoroughness and due care in decision making.

Judicial Review of Claims

Appeals of adverse decisions filed in the federal courts inevitably entail additional costs for filing fees and attorneys' time. District court judges usually assign Social Security appeals either to their law clerks or to United States magistrates. The magistrates, in turn, frequently assign such appeals to their law clerks. The law clerks and judicial officers in the federal courts merely review the cases to ensure that the ALJ's decision was supported by substantial evidence and that the correct law was applied. They do not reexamine the entire case to determine if the ALJ's judgments were correct. Because of the limited level of review applied to these cases, Social Security cases are often considered routine and tedious by decision makers within the federal courts.[35] Thus they are relegated to subordinates and thereby increase the risks of routinized, bureaucratic decision making.

A study of U.S. magistrates indicates that although some magistrates have a special interest in Social Security cases, many others consider such cases boring and burdensome. One magistrate reportedly used a checklist to have law clerks quickly affirm ALJ decisions without thoroughly reading the records of each case. Other magistrates claimed that they could decide cases merely by seeing which lawyer represented the claimant. Another magistrate claimed that he could review dozens of cases at home in a single evening, an obvious indication that the large medical record file accompanying each case was not reviewed comprehensively. Yet another magistrate was quoted as saying, "[V]irtually all Social Security appeals are from people who should never qualify."[36] These findings indicate that Social Security cases, which are usually initiated by less affluent claimants, often do not receive the same degree of care and attention as do other cases.

The Judiciary and the Politics of Social Security Disability

In 1981, the Reagan administration accelerated implementation of changes in Social Security legislation which permitted earlier and more frequent reexamination of approved claimants. Statements by Reagan administration officials indicated that the disability program had been identified as a focus for budget reduction efforts.[37] As a result of the aggressive effort to reduce the number of beneficiaries, 336,000 recipients immediately lost their eligibility for benefits. This sudden reduction in beneficiaries caused undue suffering for many disabled people. Newspaper stories documented suicides, deprivation, and disability-induced deaths suffered by former recipients as they waited for the reinstatement process to run its course.[38] As former recipients reapplied for benefits, the caseload for ALJs nearly doubled even as they experienced continuing pressures to curtail the number of approved claims. The ALJs experienced workload pressures which significantly detracted from their ability to make independent, considered judgments.

As the significant caseload increase reached the federal courts in the form of appeals, the Ninth Circuit Court of Appeals and other courts determined that a prior favorable ruling for a disability claimant created a presumption of eligibility. Thus, instead of permitting the government to withhold benefits at will in order to force beneficiaries to prove yet again that they remained disabled, the courts placed the burden on the SSA to show that each recipient's medical condition had improved before removing benefits. In effect, the circuit court rejected the Reagan administration policy of wholesale reductions in the number of beneficiaries. Instead, the court expected that the beneficiaries, all of whom had previously proven their disabled status in order to receive benefits, would be restored to the program unless the government could prove that they were no longer disabled. In response, the SSA adopted a policy of nonacquiescence in which it instructed ALJs to regard court decisions as applying only to individual cases. The SSA did not want the ALJs to follow the normal practice of regarding appellate judicial decisions as binding precedents for other cases. The SSA's policy clashed with the usual practice of respecting the legitimacy and effect of court decisions. The agency ignored the court decisions in order to force all claimants to pursue their cases through each hearing stage. The ALJs were placed in an untenable position which adversely affected claimants' opportunities to obtain deserved benefits. According to the leading study of the issue:

> If [ALJs] adhere to SSA's nonacquiescence ruling, their decisions may be overturned in Federal court because they fail to follow precedent; and if they adhere to the courts' decisions, decisions may be overturned by SSA through the Appeals Council.[39]

Although nonacquiescence policies have been practiced by the Internal Revenue Services (IRS) and the National Labor Relations Board (NLRB), the policy has had especially detrimental effects for poorer people when applied by the SSA. Unlike the IRS and NLRB cases which frequently involve an employer, union, or affluent taxpayer represented by a private attorney, disability cases affect less affluent workers who have a more difficult time pursuing their individual cases. As Susan Gluck Mezey noted in her study of the SSA's nonacquiescence policy, claimants who appealed to the courts had their benefits restored. Other claimants, who failed to appeal because of scarce resources, lack of education, or debilitating illnesses, simply lost the benefits to which they should be entitled.[40]

The federal judiciary responded to this challenge to its authority by coercing U.S. Attorneys, as officers of the court, to decline to represent the SSA's nonacquiescence position. Several judges also threatened SSA officials with contempt-of-court citations.[41] Throughout this confrontation between the judiciary and the SSA, relatively powerless former recipients bore the brunt of the nonacquiescence policy as they struggled to support themselves and their families without their deserved and accustomed disability benefits.

Although the SSA policy was eventually changed by Congress and more than 200,000 victims of the reduction policy had their benefits restored, according to Mezey, the episode illustrated the fact that courts "have only a limited capacity to coerce administrative agencies into changing public policy."[42] Thus, even in an instance in which the judiciary actively sought, on behalf of less affluent disability claimants, to countermand an agency action that contravened the law, the SSA was able to continue resistance until Congress acted. It required the aggregation of thousands of lawsuits, the mobilization of many interest groups, and a media blitz to reform the administrative policy.[43] In most instances, poor people cannot hope to gain this level of political support when they seek to change harmful practices of an administrative agency.

Administrative Adjudication and the Poor

Less affluent people are involved in administrative adjudications in contexts other than the Social Security disability program, most notably in proceedings concerning welfare benefits, workers' compensation, and employment discrimination. In all of these contexts there are significant risks that people who lack knowledge and resources will be unable to present their claims effectively. A study in the early 1970s, for example, found that welfare benefit hearings frequently did not focus on the entitlements of individual claimants. Instead, the administrative proceedings evolved into battles between agencies seeking to reduce expenditures and welfare rights organizations seeking to recruit new members and pursue policy goals.[44] In some contexts, such as Social Security disability, if claimants are aware of contingency fee arrangements, it may be possible for them to obtain professional representation. In other kinds of cases, however, this may not be feasible. Although many kinds of administrative proceedings are designed to be informal so that claimants can present their own arguments without the constraints of formal legal procedures and rules of evidence, the decision makers bear significant responsibility for ensuring that a complete record is developed. As illustrated by the Social Security disability example, pressures may be exerted upon the administrative hearing officers to conform to separate agency interests. Subsequent judicial review, if available, may not effectively ensure that the administrative proceedings were complete and proper. In sum, as with the regular court system, the less visible adjudicative proceedings within state and federal administrative agencies contain characteristics that can have detrimental consequences for less affluent people who lack the resources and education to pursue their claims effectively.

CHAPTER FIVE

The Poor and the Supreme Court

The United States Supreme Court stands literally and symbolically at the top of the American judicial system. The Supreme Court possesses the authority to reverse decisions of other courts, both state and federal, when those decisions conflict with the current constitutional and statutory interpretations of the Supreme Court majority. This chapter will focus on how the Supreme Court's processes and approaches to constitutional interpretation affect poor people.

In the course of deciding cases, the Supreme Court plays a significant role in determining public policies. Because the Supreme Court's opinions serve as binding precedents for other courts' decisions on constitutional law and federal statutes, Supreme Court cases affecting policy issues can have broad effects. The issue of school segregation provides the most famous example. The Supreme Court declared in *Brown v. Board of Education*[1] that segregation violates the Constitution. The Court subsequently endorsed the use of court-ordered busing to remedy school segregation[2] and thereby influenced the implementation of desegregation policies in hundreds of school districts. Similarly, Supreme Court decisions on criminal defendants' constitutional rights led to nationwide policies requiring police to inform suspects of their rights and to provide lawyers for indigent defendants.[3] Although chapter 6 will focus on the judiciary's broad policy-making impacts upon the poor, the specific Supreme Court procedures and theories of constitutional interpretation discussed in this chapter determine case outcomes throughout the federal courts, including cases which affect the poor.

Decision Making in the Supreme Court

Although the Supreme Court's decisions frequently follow precedents set by previous cases, constitutional law is not a fixed body of doctrine. The nine justices of the Supreme Court are the ultimate interpreters of the Constitution's meaning. The justices can follow, reverse, distinguish, or even ignore precedents in deciding new cases. Their values, ideologies, and strategic decisions affect the development of constitutional law. These same factors determine public policy outcomes including judicial policies affecting poor people. As one scholar has observed:

> [T]here exists no philosopher's stone of constitutional interpretation. Rather, it is a human process undertaken by human beings with human desires, motivations, feelings and failings. It is inevitable, then, that the Constitution will be read in the light of the philosophy of the reader, including his or her view of right and wrong, sound and unsound policy. It can be no other way.[4]

Who are these justices whose perceptions and values determine the development of constitutional law and public policy? Although some justices, such as William O. Douglas, grew up in impoverished circumstances and others, such as Louis Brandeis and Thurgood Marshall, earned reputations as lawyers representing the downtrodden, most justices came to the Supreme Court from elite backgrounds and powerful positions in politics and the legal profession.[5] As Justice Miller noted during the nineteenth century:

> It is vain to contend with judges who have been at the bar, the advocates for forty years of railroad companies, and all the forms of associated capital, when they are called upon to decide cases where such interests are in context. All their training, all their feelings are from the start in favor of those who need no such influence.[6]

In their judicial opinions, most justices have evinced little knowledge about or concern for the poor. Because the Constitution lacks explicit protections for the less affluent, the elite justices' decisions have favored other interests for most of history.

Situational Factors and Court Decisions

A scholar who examined the research studies on judicial decision making concluded that "judges' decisions are a function of what they prefer to do, tempered by what they think they ought to do, but constrained by what they perceive is feasible to do."[7] Decisions are made "within the context of group, institutional, and environmental constraints."[8] Social science research on the Supreme Court seeks to discover how case outcomes are associated with situational factors: the individual justices' attitudes and personal attributes (e.g., political party identification); the leadership role of the chief justice; strategic interactions between justices, including bargaining over votes; and historical circumstances, such as wartime decisions deferring to presidential actions despite apparent violations of the Constitution.[9]

Cases concerning poor people have sometimes been used for empirical research on the situational factors influencing Supreme Court decisions. The concern demonstrated by justices about harsh treatment of poor people has varied according to the type of issue presented in court. For example, one scholar found that:

> Empirically, evidence shows that not all justices respond in the same fashion to indigents in these two situational contexts [of welfare benefits and criminal defendants' rights]. Chief Justice [Earl] Warren, for example, was much more supportive of the right of an indigent to appeal his conviction than he was toward an indigent's right to receive welfare benefits. The much stronger support that the Court as a whole gave to the former type of grievance than it did to the latter is further evidence that the situational context affects justices' behavior.[10]

Different interpretations of the Constitution develop along with changes occurring in American society and, moreover, constitutional law changes when the composition of the Supreme Court is altered by new appointments. For example, in 1989 the Supreme Court made several decisions about abortion, affirmative action, employment discrimination, and other issues that were contrary to case precedents from the previous two decades. The words of the Constitution had not changed, but the meaning of the Constitution changed for the political reason that President Reagan appointed three members of the Court who managed to form a new majority coalition on a number of issues.

Although situational factors, historical events, and political developments influence the definition of the Constitution and the outcomes in specific cases, the justices rely upon the language of constitutional law to rationalize and legitimize their opinions. In order for their decisions to gain acceptance and legitimacy as law in the eyes of the public, the justices must take care to phrase their opinions in a manner which appears to be consistent with previous decisions, as well as with their own theories of constitutional interpretation. Thus, despite the importance of situational factors justices make efforts to develop legal doctrines that are consistent and usable by lower courts.

While these doctrines develop, change, and manifest inconsistencies because of the individual, group, and environmental factors that affect Supreme Court decisions, the Court's decisions serve to guide outcomes in lower court cases by constraining lower court judges' ability to follow their own values in deciding cases. Although the Supreme Court can ignore its own previous decisions, other courts will be reluctant to violate Supreme Court precedents because of the substantial risk that their decisions will be overturned on appeal. As a result, notwithstanding the importance of human factors in influencing Supreme Court decisions, the legal theories enunciated by the Court are important in guiding lower court decisions on a variety of matters.

Following a review of the Constitution and Supreme Court history, this chapter will examine the application of the concept of "equal protection" in order to analyze how the Supreme Court's theories of constitutional interpretation affect the interests of poor people.

The Constitution of The United States

The Framers' Protection of Property and Fear of the Masses

The Constitution was written in 1787 by a small group of affluent, politically influential men. By providing the design for the national government, including the separate powers of the legislative, executive, and judicial branches, the Constitution serves as the blueprint for the American system of government. Although the document is rightly praised for devising a workable democratic system of government, the Constitution did not notably advance the interests of poorer Americans and, in fact, many of its provisions protected the economic interests of affluent citizens. For example, the interests of slave owners were advanced by provisions which counted slaves among the population for representation in the House of Representatives, and which limited the legislature's immediate ability to regulate the importation of slaves. Other provisions preventing laws from impairing contractual obligations and requiring states to recognize each other's judicial proceedings insured that creditors could pursue debtors across state lines. These provisions favoring property owners were placed in the Constitution at a time when some poor people were mounting unsuccessful uprisings against creditors, landlords, and high taxes. For example, during Shay's Rebellion in 1786 federal troops went to Massachusetts to battle farmers who sought to fight debt proceedings and farm foreclosures.[11]

In his famous book, *An Economic Interpretation of the Constitution of the United States*, published in 1913, Charles Beard argued that the affluent framers designed the Constitution specifically to protect the economic interests of the wealthy. According to Beard, "[t]hey were anxious above everything else to safeguard the rights of private property against any leveling tendencies on the part of the propertyless masses."[12] Although Beard's controversial thesis has been attacked by historians,[13] there are clear indications that the framers sought to protect the property of affluent people while they also advanced other, less economically self-interested goals, including the creation of a workable constitutional democracy with limited governmental power.

The most obvious evidence of the framers' concerns about the preservation of wealth and property comes from James Madison's writings in *Federalist* No. 10. In explaining the benefits of creating a governing system that would minimize the destructive influences of divisive "faction[s]," Madison noted that "the most common and durable source of factions has been the various and unequal distribution of property."[14] Following the prevailing capitalist principles that have governed the American economic system since the country's beginnings, the Constitution was intended to diminish the potential for poor people or other factions formed by common interests to gain sufficient political influence to create significant changes in the economic, political, or governing systems.

According to Madison, "the first object of government" is the "protection of different and unequal faculties of acquiring property."[15] Thus, notwithstanding the obvious advantages of inheritance, political influence, and education enjoyed by affluent families for gaining and maintaining wealth, the framers of the Constitution accepted the existence of gross disparities in wealth as the natural manifestation of individuals' differing abilities. As Madison indicated, the framers viewed the protection of these advantages and attendant economic disparities as essential purposes of government.

A number of provisions of the Constitution are "undemocratic" in the sense that they prevent a majority of citizens from readily actualizing their interests through government policies. For example, although eligible citizens may vote for the president, the actual selection of the president is determined by electoral votes in the Electoral College, a procedure that guards against undesirable choices by the mass electorate. In addition, federal judges enjoy life tenure and cannot be removed from office except through the difficult impeachment process. Although both of these provisions have non-economic justifications such as, respectively, protecting against the election of a charismatic dictator and insuring the independence of the judiciary, they also effectively maintain key powers in the hands of societal elites.

Constitutional Protections and the Poor

As one scholar has noted, the ratification process for the Constitution did not create opportunities for poorer people to have their interests embodied in the document:

> If the Constitution was so blatantly elitist, how did it manage to win ratification? . . . . [T]he same superiority of wealth, organization, and control of political office and the press that allowed the rich to monopolize the Philadelphia Convention enabled them to orchestrate a successful ratification campaign. . . . What's more, *the Constitution never was submitted to a popular vote.* Ratification was by state convention composed of delegates drawn mostly from the same affluent strata as the framers. Those who voted for these delegates were themselves usually subjected to property qualifications [for eligibility to vote].[16]

By its words, the Constitution does not intend to reduce economic disparities between rich and poor. It also does not address the material deprivations of food, housing, employment opportunities, and other characteristics associated with the long-standing existence of poverty in America. Instead, the document reflects the framers' interests in preserving property rights and other aspects of a capitalist economy while creating a workable governing system based upon citizen participation and mechanisms for avoiding centralization of power, such as separation of powers and "checks and balances."

In the Bill of Rights, the first ten amendments to the Constitution which outline the rights of individuals, the document provides specific protections for all citizens regardless of economic status. The effectuation of many of these rights for poor people, however, has depended upon action by the Supreme Court. For example, until the 1960s, the Sixth Amendment's right "to have assistance of counsel for his defense" was not fully applied to state cases and effectively meant that defendants facing criminal charges could have a defense attorney *if they could afford to hire one.* Thus, even in its "neutral" provisions which were arguably not intended to favor the affluent, the Constitution did not automatically provide protection for all citizens.

The History of The Supreme Court

The Early Years: 1790 to 1865

During the first era of Supreme Court history, from the ratification of the Constitution through the Civil War, the Court's decisions focused upon defining and strengthening the American governing system. The Supreme Court clarified judicial power, presidential and congressional authority, and the distribution of legislative power between states and the federal government. Because the Court focused upon such issues as commerce power and federalism, few cases affecting the interests of poor people arrived before the Court.

In a few notable cases, during this early era, the interests of particular groups of poorer people lay beneath the legal issues presented, but the Supreme Court, in general accordance with the Constitution's lack of emphasis upon economic class disparities, did not address such interests. The 1849 case of *Luther v. Borden*,[17] for example, involved a dispute between two groups in Rhode Island, each of which claimed to be the legitimate state government. Because the Rhode Island governing system established by the 1633 royal charter remained essentially intact, wealthy people continued to control state government by reserving voting rights for those who owned substantial amounts of property. In 1841 and 1842 an alternative government was formed by citizens who believed in universal male suffrage, but their rebellion eventually collapsed. In a legal case which resulted from the dispute between the wealthy people who controlled the Rhode Island government and the poorer people seeking broader political rights, the Supreme Court declined to decide any issues, claiming that the dispute was a "political question" which should be resolved by other branches of government. By avoiding any decision, the Supreme Court effectively left the wealthy faction in control. In the 1857 decision in the *Dred Scott* case,[18] the Supreme Court rejected congressional authority to regulate slavery in the territories and declared that slaves did not have rights under the Constitution. This infamous case placed the Supreme Court squarely against the interests of a large group of poor people, namely slaves.

The Supreme Court in a Commercial Society: 1865 to 1937

After the Civil War, the Fourteenth Amendment added language to the Constitution which could provide a basis for protecting poor citizens from adverse treatment by state governments. In its most important sentence, the Fourteenth Amendment provides that:

> No state shall make or enforce any law which shall abridge the privileges or immunities of citizens of the United States; nor shall any State deprive any person of life, liberty, or property, without due process of law; nor deny to any person within its jurisdiction the equal protection of the laws.

The phrases protecting "privileges or immunities" and "equal protection" provided plausible bases for the Supreme Court to act on behalf of poor people. These appeared to be more general protections than the specific rights, such as speech and religion, which were contained in the Bill of Rights and which had little bearing upon individuals' unequal economic status within society. In important early decisions, the Supreme Court interpreted the Fourteenth Amendment very narrowly. In *The Slaughterhouse Cases* in 1873, in which butchers in New Orleans contested a government-created monopoly for slaughtering animals, the Supreme Court declined to give substantive meaning to the Privileges or Immunities Clause and declared that the Equal Protection Clause was intended only to protect the African-Americans who were recently freed from slavery.[19] Subsequent Supreme Court decisions undercut any protective power that the Fourteenth Amendment had even for African-Americans by permitting extreme racial discrimination under the transparent guise of "separate but equal" segregation[20] and by nullifying congressional attempts to permit African-Americans to fight discrimination in the courts.[21]

In addition to undercutting any potential for the Fourteenth Amendment to protect politically powerless groups, the Supreme Court shifted its attention away from individual rights and focused upon governmental efforts to initiate economic regulation and social welfare legislation. Between the Civil War and the 1930s, as the United States became increasingly industrialized, urbanized, and commercialized, various states and the federal government began to enact legislation to control business activities (e.g., regulate railroads and business monopolies) and to protect workers from harmful exploitation (e.g., minimum wage and limited weekly working hours). Although the Court upheld a few state laws,[22] as this era progressed the Supreme Court became consistently hostile to government regulations and declared hundreds of statutes to be unconstitutional. From 1888 to 1937, the Supreme Court invalidated more than four hundred state laws and seventy federal statutes.[23]

The Supreme Court generally struck down federal laws by claiming that the statutes exceeded the authority granted to Congress by the Constitution. For example, children often worked for long hours in dangerous working conditions for very low pay during this period of industrialization. In 1916 Congress sought to protect child laborers from exploitation by utilizing its power to regulate commerce in order to forbid the interstate shipment of goods produced by companies employing children under the age of fourteen.[24] In the case of *Hammer v. Dagenhart*,[25] the Supreme Court invalidated the federal Child Labor Act as exceeding congressional power under the Commerce Clause. In effect, by limiting the government's authority to regulate such activities, the Supreme Court upheld the ability of businesses to exploit poor children. Justice Oliver Wendell Holmes, in a notable dissenting opinion, lamented the fact that the Court's majority supported "the evil of premature and excessive child labor" by not permitting Congress to regulate the "product[s] of ruined lives."[26]

The Supreme Court invalidated state laws by interpreting the Fourteenth Amendment as protecting rights to economic liberty and freedom of contract which could not be infringed by state government regulation. The Court majority viewed the Due Process Clause of the Fourteenth Amendment as embodying broad economic rights which benefited business owners. Simultaneously, the Court interpreted the Equal Protection Clause and Privileges or Immunities Clause as providing virtually no protection for African-Americans, the poor, women, and other powerless groups. Although the Court claimed to be protecting the economic rights of workers, the effect was merely to protect businesses' opportunities to exploit workers without interference from government.

For example, in *Lochner v. New York*,[27] the Supreme Court invalidated a New York law which attempted to protect the health of bakery employees by limiting their working hours to ten hours per day and sixty hours per week. The majority concluded that the law interfered with the "freedom of master and employee to contract with each other" without giving any consideration to the fact that employers and employees, particularly in this era before the advent of unions, were in very unequal bargaining positions.[28] Similarly, a minimum wage law for women in New York was struck down in *Morehead v. Tipaldo*.[29] Under the guise of upholding individuals' economic liberties, these and other cases protected the interests of business by limiting states' ability to protect workers.

In the *Lochner* case, Justice Holmes dissented with the remark that "[t]he Fourteenth Amendment does not enact Mr. Herbert Spencer's Social Statics." Spencer was an influential English philosopher and sociologist whose "survival of the fittest" theory served as a popular justification for ignoring the plight of the poor. Spencer opposed any governmental intervention on behalf of the poor by declaring that:

> The whole effect of nature is to get rid of such, to clear the world of them and make room for the better. If they are sufficiently complete to live, they *do* live. If they are not, they die, and it is best that they should die.[30]

Spencer's theories were adopted not only by wealthy capitalists such as Andrew Carnegie and John D. Rockefeller, but also by Supreme Court justices such as Stephen J. Field who believed that "God intended the great to be great and the little to be little."[31]

Archibald Cox has noted how the decisions of this era merely reflected the justices' backgrounds, experiences, and beliefs. Because justices serve on the bench for life, the Supreme Court can be less sensitive than other institutions to changes occurring in American society. The opportunity to change the composition of other governmental branches every few years via elections can permit legislative and executive institutions to change more readily in response to changing societal values. As Cox observes:

> All of the Supreme Court justices who participated in the consideration of *Lochner v. New York* were born in the 1830s and 1840s. They grew up in an America ignorant of large-scale industrial organization, urban squalor, and the helplessness of the individual in dealing with organized wealth. The ideas they expressed were not unsuited to their early years [when the United States was an agrarian society]. Probably most law must lag slightly behind the march of change.[32]

The Supreme Court and Individuals' Rights: 1937 to 1990s

After clashing with President Franklin Roosevelt because of his attempts to initiate many regulatory statutes as part of his New Deal program in the 1930s, the Supreme Court accepted governmental measures affecting the economy and social welfare after Roosevelt proposed altering the size and composition of the Court. In the 1937 case of *West Coast Hotel v. Parrish,*[33] the Supreme Court approved a Washington minimum wage law. The Court subsequently accepted other state and federal statutes affecting commerce and thereby defused attacks upon the Court by the other branches of government. As Roosevelt appointees replaced members of the Supreme Court who died or retired in the late 1930s and early 1940s, the Court assumed a deferential posture toward government regulation of the economy and turned its attention to cases defining the rights of individuals under the Bill of Rights. Although the Court's changing composition influenced the new focus on individual rights, Justice Harlan Stone's famous "Footnote 4" in *United States v. Carolene Products Company*(1938) provided guidance for analyzing civil rights issues. In his famous footnote, Justice Stone argued that any legislation affecting individual rights or "discrete and insular minorities" should receive "exacting judicial scrutiny."[34]

During the 1950s and thereafter, the Supreme Court made many decisions extending constitutional protections to racial minorities, religious sects, criminal defendants, women, and other politically weak groups. It was during this period that the Court began to address specifically issues concerning the legal protections afforded to poor people under the Constitution.

The Supreme Court and Equal Protection Analysis

The Fourteenth Amendment provision prohibiting states from denying people "equal protection of the laws" created the first explicit basis for preventing formal discrimination by government. Because the Supreme Court declared in *The Slaughterhouse Cases* (1873) that the Equal Protection Clause applied only to African-Americans, the provision's initial potential for redressing discrimination against various groups in society was significantly diminished. Although the Court struck down a few discriminatory laws, until the 1950s the Supreme Court effectively nullified the Equal Protection Clause by permitting discrimination against African-Americans on a massive scale through the "separate but equal" doctrine. The Court failed to examine the fact that racial segregation inevitably led to grossly unequal treatment. After a series of legal challenges to inequality in higher education during the 1930s and 1940s demonstrated that "separate but equal" was a sham, the Supreme Court eventually gave meaning to the Equal Protection Clause in *Brown v. Board of Education* (1954) by unanimously declaring that racially separate schools are inherently unequal and unconstitutional.

The Development of Tests for Equal Protection Violations

The Supreme Court developed a framework for analyzing discrimination claims under the Equal Protection Clause that adhered to Justice Stone's exhortation in "Footnote Four" to give closer scrutiny to governmental actions impinging upon individuals' rights. Under Equal Protection Analysis, for certain issues the Court applies "strict scrutiny" by asking whether the discriminatory regulation is *necessarily related to a compelling governmental interest.* The two categories of issues which elicit this exacting analysis are regulations which discriminate according to "suspect classifications" (e.g., race) and those which impinge upon "fundamental rights." In other words, if someone alleges discriminatory action by government and further claims that the discrimination is based upon a suspect classification or that it violates a fundamental right, then the state must show that

its regulation is the only means to achieve some supremely important governmental goal. Because the Court's level of scrutiny is so
strict, it is extremely difficult for a state law or policy to survive if it
collides with a suspect classification or fundamental right. For example, a state would have to demonstrate a compelling reason to provide
explicitly different governmental services to members of various racial groups. It is extremely difficult to conceive of a reason that would
justify such differential treatment by race. It is up to the Court, however, to determine whether a suspect classification or fundamental
right is at issue in each particular case.

If a governmental action treats people differently, but does not
impinge upon a fundamental right or does not implicate a suspect
classification, then the Court merely examines the statute to see if it
is *rationally related to a legitimate state interest.* This is a very low
level of scrutiny so that virtually any statute can survive so long as it
is rational and the government can legitimately pursue the object of
the statute's purpose. For example, a law requiring airline pilots to
pass eye examinations at a higher standard than those imposed for
automobile drivers would clearly discriminate against pilots by plac-
ing a greater burden upon them. However, because there is no fundamental constitutional right to fly airplanes and airline pilots are not a
suspect classification, the law would be approved as a rational means
to advance the legitimate governmental interest in aviation safety.
The discrimination against pilots would not implicate a suspect classification because the Court has reserved that designation and level
of constitutional protection for groups that suffer from "invidious"
discrimination, namely unfair, harmful actions which stem from ill
will or prejudice. In regard to the Equal Protection Clause and poor
people, the Supreme Court has been confronted with the question
whether statutes affecting the poor implicate a suspect classification
or whether such statutes impinge upon fundamental rights. If the
Court does not find the existence of either of those two conditions,
then the poor are denied constitutional protection from discriminatory government laws and policies.

Because *The Slaughterhouse Cases* initially established that the
Equal Protection Clause applied only to African-Americans, the justices were not inclined to apply equal protection principles for the
benefit of other groups.[35] Even after the Supreme Court's attention
turned to the constitutional rights of individuals during the twentieth century, the movement toward expanding the coverage of the
Equal Protection Clause was very slow until the 1960s. For example,
in 1948, a majority on the Court approved a Michigan statute that

prohibited women from working as bartenders unless they were the wives or daughters of tavern owners.[36] Justice Felix Frankfurter acknowledged that the Equal Protection Clause "precludes irrational discrimination as between persons or groups of persons in the incidence of a law." Although he therefore implicitly accepted that women could be protected from unequal treatment, he readily accepted Michigan's paternalistic justifications for selectively shielding women, but not men, from the evils associated with liquor establishments. The Supreme Court applied strict scrutiny to discriminatory racial classifications after *Brown v. Board of Education*, but the application of such protections to other categories of victimized people has been limited and inconsistent.

In a 1941 case affecting poor people, California prosecuted a man who brought his unemployed brother-in-law to that state from Texas.[37] California law made it a misdemeanor to bring an indigent person into the state with knowledge of that persons's indigent status. California claimed the law was to protect the state's social, moral, and financial stability, but obviously the law fell very harshly upon poor people who wished to move to California in order to seek work in the state's rapidly expanding economy. The Supreme Court invalidated the California law on the grounds that only Congress could regulate interstate commerce and the transportation of people constituted "commerce." Although a transportation company, such as a railroad or passenger bus company, clearly transports people for commercial purposes, this application of interstate commerce analysis to private citizens transporting their relatives practically equates people with property, as if human beings are merely objects in the control of other people. Moreover, despite several concurring opinions arguing that the law violated poor individuals' rights to travel or "privileges and immunities of citizenship" under the Fourteenth Amendment, the majority gave no serious consideration to the issue of poor people's constitutional rights. The Court ignored the obvious implications for Equal Protection Clause considerations about discrimination against indigent people.

The Supreme Court used strict scrutiny analysis under the Equal Protection Clause to invalidate many laws based upon racial classifications. However, aside from race and national origin, two categories that virtually everyone would agree are "suspect," the Supreme Court has not systematically protected anyone else from discriminatory regulations. In some circumstances the Supreme Court has applied strict scrutiny for situationally defined suspect classifications and for fundamental rights. For example, the Court regarded alienage (i.e., foreign citizenship) as a suspect classification in invalidating state laws requiring United States citizenship for welfare benefits[38] and for admission to the legal profession.[39] In other situations, however, the Court rejected strict scrutiny analysis in approving citizenship requirements for police officers.[40] Since the late 1960s, the Court generally has regarded illegitimacy (i.e. offspring of unmarried parents) as a suspect classification. Although the justices invalidated inheritance and workers' compensation statutes that discriminated in the distribution of benefits against children born out of wedlock,[41] they also approved an inheritance statute that placed priority on the interests of legitimate children.[42]

The Supreme Court has been divided over gender as a suspect classification. Although Chief Justice William Rehnquist regards gender discrimination as, unlike racial discrimination, not deserving any special attention under the Equal Protection Clause, other members of the Court disagree. Initially, only four justices regarded gender as a suspect classification.[43] As an apparent compromise in a subsequent case concerning discrimination against young males under Oklahoma's law governing the legal drinking age, one of those four justices, Justice William Brennan, created a new, middle-level of scrutiny for cases of gender discrimination.[44] This new standard gained the support of a majority of the Court. Brennan's standard, which has been applied in subsequent cases, provides that governmental regulations that discriminate by gender must be *substantially related to important governmental objectives.* Thus gender receives less judicial attention than race, which requires a demonstration of "compelling" government interests, but it merits greater scrutiny than most categories which receive a mere rationality test.

The Poor and Equal Protection

The Supreme Court initially gave indications that it might regard wealth discrimination as implicating a suspect classification. The Supreme Court held in 1956 that states must provide trial transcripts free of charge to indigent defendants wishing to appeal their convictions.[45] In 1966, the Court struck down statutes that conditioned voting eligibility upon payment of a poll tax.[46] A few years later, the Court invalidated a state residency requirement for welfare benefits.[47] Although Chief Justice Earl Warren used language which indicated that wealth, like race, was a factor "which independently render[s] a classification highly suspect,"[48] the decisions protecting poor people under Equal Protection analysis were actually justified on the basis of protecting specific fundamental rights rather than scrutinizing wealth as a suspect classification. The fundamental rights protected in the foregoing examples were, respectively, the rights to have access to the courts, to vote, and to travel.

The Court never explicitly declared that wealth discrimination deserved the exacting "strict scrutiny" analysis applied to discrimination cases involving suspect classifications such as race and national origin. The Court also never explicitly equated wealth discrimination with gender discrimination which received mid-level scrutiny by the justices. In 1973, the issue became settled when a slim five-member majority declared that wealth differentiation did not involve any suspect classification.[49] Thus poor people would receive the benefits of strict Equal Protection analysis only when specific fundamental rights were violated. In other instances it would be permissible for states' policies to discriminate against the poor for merely rational as opposed to compelling reasons. For example, the Supreme Court found that although school financing systems based upon property taxes generate unequal educational resources for children living in areas with lower property values, because the poor are not a suspect classification and there is no constitutional right to education, property taxes are acceptable as a rational means to finance schools.[50] In this education discrimination case in which poor parents challenged the Texas school financing system, Texas conceded that its property tax methods would be unconstitutional if the Supreme Court chose to apply strict scrutiny by recognizing the poor as a suspect classification or by recognizing education as a fundamental right.[51]

Although the poor do not benefit from strict scrutiny analysis under the Equal Protection Clause, the Supreme Court has invalidated several detrimental laws that impinge upon fundamental rights such as voting. In addition, as chapter 6 will discuss, in some cases involving welfare benefits, the Court has provided protections for the poor, but usually under the guise of some separate right, such as the right to travel. Some observers have compared the protection against wealth discrimination to the middle-level protection provided against gender discrimination.[52] The mixed results of cases, however, have led other observers to conclude that the Court will apply the Equal Protection Clause to the poor only when it can link the asserted claims against discriminatory policies to some perceived fundamental right.[53]

Why should the poor be excluded from the highest protections of strict Equal Protection analysis? Discrimination against the poor can be invidious, based upon prejudice, and have significantly harmful effects upon people's lives. If one interpreted the Constitution narrowly, according to the original intentions of the Fourteenth Amendment's authors, then perhaps there could be an argument that the Equal Protection Clause was only meant to forbid racial discrimination. However, because the Supreme Court has expanded Equal Protection to encompass discrimination based upon gender, alienage, and illegitimacy, there is no principled reason to deny protection to people who are victimized by governmental discrimination because of their economic status.

In an insightful analysis of the Supreme Court's approach to the Equal Protection Clause, Michael McCann noted that the Court needlessly attempts to reserve protection for "discrete and insular minority" *groups.*[54] Because definitions of poverty are subject to dispute and poor individuals have diverse characteristics, justices have argued that there is no specific group called "the poor" to be protected. Equal Protection analysis, however, could easily be applied to protect individuals from discrimination because any challenged statute that discriminated on the basis of wealth would affect an identifiable number of people whether or not it encompassed an entire group that could be labeled "the poor." For example, in the Texas school financing case, the Court could have recognized that all children in poorer districts were deprived of "equal protection" in the form of inequitable educational resources without seeking to find any other characteristics (e.g., race, national origin) to link these victims together as a more discrete, identifiable group. The group was both identifiable and victimized because of the dividing line between school districts created by education financing law.

Moreover, McCann documents how Supreme Court justices appear to believe that poor people are responsible for their own status in society and could readily alter their membership among "the poor." As a result, according to McCann:

> [S]tate policies that have discriminatory impacts upon the poor are not "suspect" because they tend less to inhibit access to social opportunity than to merely recognize the "natural" personal inequalities of ability, character, and motivation . . . which [the] government, like the market, is not constitutionally obliged to remedy.[55]

These views are, as McCann persuasively argues, "rooted more in fantasy than in fact."[56] Any realistic assessment of American society would indicate that "[w]idespread poverty, unemployment, and worker powerlessness are enduring aspects of our long-developing capitalist legacy; they are as stable in character and degree as they are resistant to liberal reformist political tinkering."[57] Most people born into poverty in the United States will remain in the underclass because the attributes of affluence which they lack, such as quality educational opportunities and access to high-paying jobs, play such a significant role in determining people's careers and material success. Even if everyone, rich and poor, pushed themselves to attend college or to gain a technical skill, the American economy does not have enough high-paying jobs to pull everyone out of poverty. Some people would still work for minimum wage at McDonald's and some would still be unemployed. In other words, contrary to the prevailing American ideology and the Supreme Court's assumptions, the existence of poverty is affected by the structure of the American economy and is not simply determined by individuals' personal characteristics.

Archibald Cox argues that the Supreme Court has backed away from applying the Equal Protection Clause fully to issues of wealth discrimination because the Court is afraid of confrontations with other branches of government. According to Cox, rather than merely order government or businesses not to discriminate, as in racial and gender discrimination cases, recognition of wealth as a suspect classification would lead the Court to order the implementation of expensive public policies to equalize treatment between rich and poor, such as ordering states to provide equal funding for rich and poor school districts. The Court would risk its legitimacy if it ordered the states or Congress to increase taxes and create new programs, because the other governmental branches might refuse to obey.[58]

Although Cox is correct in observing that such orders affecting public policies would risk confrontations with other governmental units, the federal judiciary has undertaken such confrontations before, most notably in remedying school segregation. Many school districts stalled and resisted implementation of school desegregation orders, but the federal government eventually used its resources and power to assist in implementing court orders. In the end, the Court retained its legitimacy as a respected judicial institution despite its unpopular decisions supporting busing. Moreover, a recent historical study of the Supreme Court indicates that the institution is less vulnerable to political opposition than many political scientists have always assumed.[59]

As chapter 6 will discuss in specific areas of law, the Supreme Court has developed a narrow interpretation of the Equal Protection Clause which generally permits governmental policies to discriminate against poor people. The words and meaning of the Fourteenth Amendment do not compel the Court to exclude poor people from protection under the Equal Protection Clause. The prevailing views about poverty, however, affect the elite lawyers who become justices and influence their decidedly unsympathetic outlook toward the poor. As Stumpf has noted, "American society has never decided, even symbolically, that poverty is wrong and that market conditions helping to create and perpetuate it are legally correctable."[60]

Supreme Court Processes

In order for a case to receive consideration by the Supreme Court, it must meet the Court's jurisdictional requirements. For example, it must be a genuine controversy between two parties and not a "friendly" lawsuit designed to develop new law. The proper parties who have actually suffered injuries must initiate the action. This rule requiring "standing" in order to sue has limited the ability of interest groups to assist poor people in some cases. In addition, a case must have been reviewed by the highest possible prior court, usually either a U.S. Court of Appeals or a state supreme court, before the U.S. Supreme Court will consider it. This requirement inevitably means that cases arriving at the Supreme Court have already been considered by two or three prior courts. Thus, taking a case all the way to the Supreme Court necessitates the significant time and expense of pursuing litigation through each stage of a state or federal court system. The many jurisdictional requirements could easily discourage litigants who lack the resources, patience, or will to push a case continually through numerous hearings over a period of several years.

The Supreme Court has virtually complete control over the cases that it will hear. Whether cases arrive at the Court through appeal or, more usually, through a writ of certiorari asking the justices to order that the record of a case be sent up from a lower court, four justices must vote to hear a case in order for it to be considered by the Court. Normally the justices can give full hearings to only about 150 out of the more than 4,000 cases filed with the Court each year. Another 150 to 200 may be disposed of through a summary decision, but more than 90 percent of petitions are denied any review by the justices.

Petitioners must pay a $200 fee when they file for consideration by the Supreme Court and an additional $100 if the case is accepted for hearing. These fees are in addition to fees that have already been paid at each preceding court in which the case was considered. About half of the petitions to the Supreme Court are filed *in forma pauperis*, meaning that the petitioner claims to be too poor to pay the fee and therefore requests to have the fee waived. About eighty percent of these "paupers' petitions" are filed by prisoners in state and federal correctional facilities. Unlike the paid cases which are reviewed by law clerks working for all of the justices, until the 1970s the paupers' cases were evaluated by the chief justice's law clerks. The other justices received summaries only of those cases that the chief justice's office believed might merit attention. This created an obvious risk that paupers' petitions might not receive the same consideration as other cases. Despite changes to insure that all petitions are reviewed in the same manner, petitions filed by poor litigants have a significantly lower likelihood of being accepted by the Supreme Court than do cases from petitioners who can afford to pay the fees. For example, during 1986–1987 the Supreme Court accepted fewer than 1 percent of paupers' cases while accepting 12 percent of paid cases.[61]

The differences in acceptance rates may be attributable to the poor quality of argument by indigent petitioners who lack legal assistance and therefore do not know how to identify and present proper constitutional arguments. However, because acceptance of cases is based upon discretionary judgments by the justices and their assistants, some favoritism might exist for paid cases. The justices attempt to select cases of the greatest importance, including cases that will advance the development of constitutional and federal law in directions commensurate with the individual justices' preferences. Because of the justices' general lack of interest in issues affecting the poor, as illustrated by their narrow application of the Equal Protection Clause, cases involving poor people may not fare as well in the evaluation process. As one important scholar commented on the Supreme Court's selection of cases during the 1970s and 1980s, "a majority of the Burger Court, unlike the Warren Court [during the 1960s], is unsympathetic to claims brought by indigents."[62]

Representation and the Costs of Supreme Court Litigation

If the Supreme Court decides to hear a case submitted by someone who cannot afford the filing fee, the Court will appoint an attorney to represent the petitioner. An excellent description of the process through which an indigent petitioner's claim succeeded in the nation's highest court is presented in Gideon's Trumpet.[63] Gideon's Trumpet presents a detailed account of an indigent prisoner's efforts to establish that all criminal defendants facing imprisonment should be entitled to the assistance of an attorney whether or not they can afford to pay for counsel. The Supreme Court accepted Gideon's case in the early 1960s because a majority of justices were prepared to change the law defining criminal defendants' right to representation. After deciding that Gideon's case would be the proper vehicle for changing their interpretation of the Constitution, the justices appointed the best counsel available, distinguished lawyer and future Supreme Court justice Abe Fortas, to represent Gideon. When the Supreme Court selected his case as a vehicle for changing the law, Gideon enjoyed the same advantages as the wealthiest litigants by having a resource-rich, high-powered law firm working on his case.

The costs of litigation are substantial. Normally it would cost tens of thousands of dollars in attorneys' fees to pursue a case all the way to the Supreme Court. If litigants are indigent, they can seek to have the filing fees waived and can assume that the Court will appoint attorneys to take the cases if the petitions are accepted. But what if a litigant can afford the filing fees and some attorneys' fees, but does not have adequate resources to pay the thousands of dollars necessary to carry a case through to the Supreme Court? There is a great likelihood that, as with civil litigation in general, the length and cost of the process will eventually compel people to settle or to surrender their claims. Wealthy people can afford to seek further court reviews all the way to the Supreme Court. Indigent people have nothing to lose by filing petitions themselves and seeking to have fees waived. People who are not indigent, however, whether they are working poor people or middle-class people, have a very difficult time sustaining the burden of litigation costs, even in cases in which they have strong legal justifications for pursuing their claims.

If litigants' cases present novel or important issues that fit with the political agenda of an interest group, they may be fortunate enough to receive free legal assistance from professional litigators. Interest group litigation became a favored strategy of various political organizations, both liberal and conservative, as a legacy of the NAACP's success in presenting cases that struck down the legal basis for school segregation in the 1950s and 1960s. Because of the expense of significant cases, such as the Dayton, Ohio, school desegregation litigation which cost the plaintiffs nearly $2 million to pursue,[64] few individuals could sustain the legal effort needed to bring cases repeatedly before the Supreme Court. Interest groups possess quite limited resources so they carefully select only a few cases to pursue regardless of the existence of other legitimate claims that are worthy of representation.

Congress has attempted to increase the availability of resources through the Civil Rights Attorneys Fees Act and the Access to Justice Act which provide for payment of attorneys' fees to the prevailing parties in certain circumstances. However, a poor litigant must convince an attorney to assume the risk of undertaking the case before knowing whether the litigation will succeed and whether the case will subsequently meet the requirements to qualify for payment of fees. Because of the Supreme Court's lack of interest in issues affecting the poor, attorneys generally will be cautious about assuming the risk of representing poor people. Even if the cases present legitimate issues and arguments, the Supreme Court's current refusal to recognize protections for poor people will probably diminish the chances for any eventual success and compensation, and thereby deter lawyers from accepting such cases.

Conclusion

As the "living voice of the Constitution,"[65] the Supreme Court serves as a symbol of law and justice. As with all human political institutions, however, the Court is influenced by historical developments, prevailing ideologies, and individual actors' values and attitudes. The history of the Supreme Court indicates that its function has been, in the characterization of Yale professor Robert Dahl, "to confer legality and constitutionality on the fundamental policies of the successful [political] coalition [that controls the institutions of government]."[66] The Supreme Court generally has advanced and maintained the goals of the affluent interests that dominate American politics without giving much consideration to the problems of poverty and poor people. Although the Court, according to Dahl, "sometimes serves as a guide and even a pioneer in arriving at different standards of fair play and individual right than have resulted, or are likely to result, from the interplay of the other political forces,"[67] this leadership role has focused upon issues of racial discrimination rather than upon poverty or wealth discrimination. As chapter 6 will discuss in regard to various policy issues, the Supreme Court has advanced limited constitutional protections for the poor in the context of specific rights (e.g., criminal defendants' rights), but constitutional law has not served as a vehicle to alter the broader detrimental consequences of economic inequality within American society.

CHAPTER SIX

The Courts and Public Policy

O ne of the recognized functions of courts is policy making. In its most general sense, policy making can be regarded, in the words of Lawrence Baum, as "the establishment and application of authoritative rules."[1] As one of the three branches of government, the judiciary provides a forum in which people can seek to advance their goals for directing governmental actions and allocating resources within society. Groups and individuals who lack the political power to influence the policy-making decisions of legislatures and executive branch officials may present their policy objectives as legal claims in order to seek assistance from judges.

Courts as Policymakers

Judicial policy making can result from judges' opinions interpreting either constitutional provisions or statutes. Because the judiciary possesses primary authority over constitutional interpretation, policy outcomes stemming from such decisions are less susceptible, although not immune, to direct counteraction by other branches of government. By contrast, when judges' policy-making decisions are based upon their ability to interpret and define statutes, legislatures can override the judicial determinations by rewriting and clarifying the statutes. For example, Title IX of the Education Amendments of 1972 prohibited gender discrimination in any educational program receiving federal funds. The Supreme Court interpreted the law very narrowly to permit a college to limit its nondiscrimination policy to the office directly receiving the government money, namely the financial aid office.[2] Critics of the Court's decision claimed that Congress actually intended for the antidiscrimination law to cover entire educational institutions, rather than merely apply to specific offices within colleges. Congress subsequently passed the Civil Rights Restoration Act of 1988 to override the Court's decision by specifically requiring that institutions receiving federal funds implement institution-wide nondiscrimination policies. Thus, judicial policy determinations relying upon statutory interpretation place courts in an interactive yet potentially subordinate relationship with legislatures.

The Legitimacy of Courts as Policymakers

Based upon their unique authority to define federal and state constitutions, judges may issue decisions affecting public policies. These decisions can raise serious questions about the legitimacy and capacity of courts to make appropriate policy decisions within a democratic system of government. Judicial decisions affecting discrimination, pornography, freedom of speech, abortion, and other controversial issues are based upon constitutional interpretation and therefore, unlike cases of statutory interpretation, cannot be readily countermanded by other branches of government.

Within many state court systems, people can influence and reject controversial judicial decisions by simply voting for different judges during the next election. In the federal system, however, because judges are appointed to serve "during good Behaviour,"[3] which can effectively mean lifetime tenure, there is no direct accountability to the voters or elected branches of government. Federal judges are granted lifetime appointments, subject only to removal through impeachment for serious misconduct, in order to insulate them from political influences and to encourage courageous, fair decisions. Yet, such terms in office conflict with an underlying assumption of democracy that requires the citizenry to control government and policy making. Thus, policy decisions from the courts, especially those dictating specific expenditures of state or federal government funds, elicit complaints that federal judges behave as undemocratic "dictators." However, a number of practical factors limit the potential for judicial abuse of policy-making power.

One factor which limits the dictatorial potential of federal judges is the political nature of the judicial system. The judges do not make decisions in isolation. They are drawn from the elite, politically powerful segments of society so that their values, attitudes, and decisions are frequently in step with the decisions of the similarly elite elected officials. In the hierarchy of the court system, appellate courts and the Supreme Court maintain a check on any "maverick" lower court judges by reversing overreaching decisions.

Political science research indicates that judges may restrain their own decision-making power because they believe the judiciary should play a limited role in policy making or because they perceive that they lack the power to enforce broad policy decisions.[4] Unlike legislative and executive branches, judges control no taxing power or military forces with which to pressure recalcitrant officials and the public into complying with judicial policy decisions. In fact, in a decision in 1990, the Supreme Court specifically limited the ability of federal judges to impose fines upon public officials who disobey judicial orders.[5] Because they possess limited enforcement powers, judges generally rely upon voluntary acquiescence motivated by respect for and acceptance of the courts as legitimate legal institutions. Such acceptance could conceivably be jeopardized by excessively controversial or far-reaching policy decisions. In addition, the judiciary is limited by significant political influences exercised by the legislative and executive branches of government. For example, Congress can initiate laws limiting or removing the courts' jurisdiction over certain issues and the president can alter the composition of the courts, as President Reagan did during the 1980s, by appointing new judges and justices who possess different values and policy goals. Thus several political factors limit the practical threat of a dictatorial judiciary.

Judicial Policy Making and Democracy

Are federal judges really potential "dictators" and hence illegitimate policymakers in a democratic system of government? Fundamentally, the answer to this question depends upon one's definition of democracy. If one defines democracy as direct citizen control over government and policy making, then important governmental decisions should be made by the branches directly accountable to the people, namely, the elected officials in the legislative and executive branches. However, if one defines democracy as citizen control over government and public policy *plus* protection of rights for political minorities, then there is necessarily a role for an independent judiciary as the enforcer of constitutional rules and, simultaneously, an influence on public policies.

For example, if all policy-making power resided in elected branches of government, there would be a risk of "tyranny of the majority" as majoritarian political interests shape public policies to the detriment of minority racial, gender, religious, and other groups who lack political power. Because the United States Constitution provides specific protections for individuals in the Bill of Rights and other constitutional amendments, it is clear that the American governing system is designed to limit the absolute control of public policy by political majorities. Thus judges are responsible for ensuring that despised criminal defendants receive certain rights in the criminal justice process; racial minorities can exercise their right to vote; small church groups can undertake their religious practices; communists and other political outcasts can give speeches; and other groups and individuals who lack political power are not overwhelmed by the policy goals of the majority.

Because poor people, as a minority of the population, lack political power, they also risk detrimental treatment at the hands of political majorities in the legislative and executive branches of government. Indeed, there are many examples of tax laws and other legislative policies that clearly favor politically powerful affluent people.[6] Although they are not always recognized as such, poor people constitute a political minority group eligible for protection by judges. This chapter will discuss areas in which judicial policy making has affected poor people.

The Courts and Social Change

During the 1950s and 1960s, the U.S. Supreme Court issued a number of decisions expanding the scope of individuals' rights under the Constitution. The Court's rulings against racial discrimination in education, voting, and other spheres of American life coincided with increased political activity by civil rights groups seeking to eliminate racial inequality. Following the Supreme Court's lead, the federal judiciary became more receptive to claims by individuals against government. Members of various groups which lacked political power in the majoritarian electoral processes controlling legislative and executive branches of government saw judges as saviors who could redress inequality and injustice. Racial minorities, religious groups, women, prisoners, disabled people, and others utilized litigation to seek recognition of constitutional protections and to change public policies.

Disadvantaged groups developed an optimistic, naive faith in the willingness and power of courts to redress societal inequalities through reliance on flexible constitutional principles of justice. Stuart Scheingold characterized the beliefs that everyone receives a fair hearing in court and that judges' orders are effective instruments of social change as components of a "myth of rights" that permeates the political orientations of claimants.[7] The Supreme Court served as a focal point for this faith in constitutional litigation, although in the aftermath of adverse decisions by Reagan appointees in the late 1980s, many civil rights groups have subsequently recognized that the Court does not provide a dependable and stable source of support.[8]

The Poor and the "Myth of Rights"

Because of courts' limited ability to enforce judicial orders, many important decisions are primarily symbolic statements by judges which influence subsequent political developments in society. *Brown v. Board of Education* (1954) is regarded as a monumental declaration against racial discrimination in education. However, schools remained segregated throughout the country following the decision because court decrees are not self-executing. As previously discussed, judges have relatively little direct power to force immediate compliance. Segregation was altered in many school districts, but only through subsequent suits and legislative actions over a twenty-year period after *Brown*. As with other societal problems brought to the judiciary for redress, social change did not occur simply because of court decisions. According to Scheingold, "it was not the decisions themselves but the political mobilization spawned by *resistance* to the decisions that brought positive results."[9]

This link between judicial decisions and political mobilization has produced few benefits for the poor. As subsequent sections of this chapter will discuss, there have been few judicial decisions basing symbolic declarations upon recognition that poor people constitute an identifiable, unfairly disadvantaged group. By contrast, there have been many decisions concerning racial and gender discrimination which have helped to mobilize political action and social change. Even if the courts issued rulings supporting rights for the poor, poor people would have less ability to capitalize upon these symbolic declarations in order to achieve political gains. Unlike the case of poor people, other groups, such as racial minorities and women, contain lawyers and other professionals with political skills who can generate and maintain litigation, lobby legislatures and executive agencies, and undertake other activities to influence public policy. During the twentieth century, poor people have mobilized briefly over specific issues such as employment opportunities and welfare rights, but as Frances Fox Piven and Richard Cloward have demonstrated, such political movements have failed for lack of resources and momentum.[10]

Access to Justice

One area in which the U.S. Supreme Court has received credit for evincing sensitivity to the disadvantages experienced by poor people is in access to the courts. Because the judiciary constitutes one of the three branches of government and, more particularly, because judicial institutions bear a special responsibility for protecting the constitutional rights of people who lack political power, there are strong reasons for judges to ensure that less affluent people receive adequate legal resources and attention. Judicial policy decisions ordering the provision of legal resources for poor people generated opposition from state governments that did not wish to expend public funds on ensuring access to the courts for less affluent people. Although the court decisions providing access to justice have reduced some gross inequalities, as discussed in chapters 2 and 3, poor people still suffer detrimental effects in both criminal and civil justice from inadequate legal resources. Moreover, the judicial decisions providing access and resources to less affluent people have been relatively limited in scope, especially in regard to civil court proceedings.

Access to Justice in Criminal Courts

As discussed in chapter 2, the Sixth Amendment guarantee of a right to counsel had no practical meaning for poor defendants until the middle of the twentieth century. In the 1930s and 1940s, the Supreme Court began to apply the right to counsel to state criminal proceedings by requiring that indigent defendants be given defense attorneys in death penalty cases[11] and when defendants were uneducated, illiterate, or otherwise especially unable to represent themselves in court.[12]

The Supreme Court took a major step against wealth discrimination in the criminal justice system with its decision in *Griffin v. Illinois*[13] in 1956. In guaranteeing that indigent defendants receive free trial transcripts in order to prepare their appeals, Justice Hugo Black wrote: "In criminal trials a State can no more discriminate on account of poverty than on account of religion, race, or color. . . . There can be no equal justice where the kind of trial a man gets depends on the amount of money he has."[14] Although Black's opinion was joined by only three other colleagues and therefore his stirring rhetoric did not create binding precedent, the *Griffin* decision ushered in an era in which the Court made several decisions ensuring that poor people gained access to judicial resources. These decisions abolished filing fee barriers for defendants seeking to appeal convictions and undertake other post-conviction proceedings,[15] and eventually led to cases providing defense attorneys for indigents.

In the 1963 case of *Gideon v. Wainwright*[16] the Supreme Court required that states provide defense attorneys for all indigent defendants who face at least six months imprisonment. Archibald Cox has called the *Gideon* decision "the single most important reform" of criminal defendants' rights initiated by the Supreme Court.[17] In a subsequent case, *Argersinger v. Hamlin*, the *Gideon* principle was extended to all cases in which the defendant's punishment following conviction involved incarceration of any length.[18] The *Gideon* decision helped to redress a significant imbalance within the criminal justice system by mitigating the courtroom mismatch between a professional prosecutor with all of the state's resources on one side and a poor, frequently uneducated defendant on the other. Although the outcomes of most criminal cases are determined through plea bargaining, poor defendants gained assistance in obtaining equitable plea agreements. Obviously, as chapter 2 indicated, the interposition of defense counsel does not guarantee equal or even adequate representation. Despite the problems associated with appointed counsel for poor defendants, the *Gideon* case represented a significant advance toward greater equality in representation and in access to judicial resources.

The Supreme Court made additional decisions advancing equal access to the courts by ensuring that indigent defendants receive an attorney during police interrogations[19] and during initial appeals granted as a matter of right under state law.[20] The development of cases advancing equal access to judicial resources came to a halt as the composition of the Supreme Court changed because of the retirements of justices from the era of Chief Justice Earl Warren and the addition of Nixon appointees. For example, in 1974 the Court determined that indigent defendants are not entitled to the assistance of counsel in preparing permissive appeals. In the Court's opinion, Chief Justice Burger would concede only that "indigent defendant[s] [are] *somewhat* handicapped in comparison with a wealthy defendant who has counsel . . . at every stage in the proceeding"[21] (emphasis added). Burger's modest admission seriously understates the mismatch between untrained criminal defendants pursuing appeals and professional lawyers representing the state. There is no doubt that the lack of professional assistance in identifying appealable issues and in complying with technical legal requirements for appeals significantly disadvantages poor defendants who must attempt to undertake legal research and writing for themselves.

Chief Justice Burger declared that limitations must be placed upon judicial decisions leading to equalized treatment in society because "there are obviously limits beyond which the equal protection analysis may not be pressed without doing violence to principles recognized in other decisions of this Court."[22] Although the Chief Justice did not specify what principles would be violated by advancing equal access to judicial resources for the poor, presumably he was re-

luctant to impose upon state governments the costs of providing resources to indigent defendants. Policy-making decisions by judges inevitably affect both the decision-making ability of other
governmental officials and the allocation of public funds. In seeking
to limit the recognition of rights for criminal defendants, the Burger-
era appointees placed great emphasis upon restraining judicial policy
making affecting poor defendants' access to justice. These justices
sought to defer to the decisions by elected officials in state and federal
government. This formulation of the appropriate role for judges reflected a conception of democracy that placed less emphasis than
their Warren-era predecessors upon the protection of individuals'
rights. As a result, the decisions of the Burger era, although not reversing the protections established during the Warren era, limited
the judicial resources provided to poor defendants and thereby pre-
served many inequalities based upon wealth.

In 1979, the four Nixon appointees were joined by Justices
Byron White and Potter Stewart in sharply limiting the availability
of legal counsel for the poor. In the case of *Scott v. Illinois*, a defendant was convicted of theft and, although he faced the possibility of
one year in jail, his sentence was a $50 fine.[23] The Court determined
that the indigent petitioner was not entitled to counsel unless he
was actually sentenced to incarceration. Thus, if the ultimate punishment for a criminal offense is merely a fine, there is no constitutional right to counsel. Although Justice Rehnquist admitted that
he lacked empirical evidence to demonstrate how costly it would be
for states to provide representation for all indigent defendants, he
justified the *Scott* decision by declaring that "any extension [of
Argersinger] would create confusion and impose unpredictable, but
necessarily substantial, costs on fifty quite diverse states."[24] The
dissenters refuted Rehnquist's "alarmist prophecies that [provision
of counsel] would wreak havoc on the States" by demonstrating
that Scott would have already been entitled to counsel in at least
thirty-three states under existing state laws.[25] The balance Rehnquist struck in favoring states' economic interests over poor defendants' representation in criminal court implied that mere fines are
not a punishment worthy of concern. However, any criminal conviction, even if punished by probation or fines, carries with it
stigma and a criminal record which may have devastating effects
upon a poor defendant's ability to obtain employment and credit.
Unlike individuals affluent enough to obtain their own defense lawyers, poor people who face minor criminal charges without representation incur risks of lifelong detrimental consequences resulting
from unwarranted criminal convictions.

Access to Justice in Civil Courts

In the civil context, there is no protection comparable to the Sixth Amendment's limited right to counsel for indigent criminal defendants. In order for citizens to utilize the judicial branch to seek compensation for a personal injury, enforce a contract, or pursue some other civil legal matter, aggrieved parties must obtain their own legal counsel. This inequality in access to legal resources necessarily disadvantages poor people who would like to seek remedies for their grievances in the courts.

If the potential recovery from a civil case is sufficiently high, an attorney may accept the case without charge in anticipation of drawing a 30-percent contingency fee off the top of any settlement or favorable judgment. In more modest civil cases, a poor claimant may be entitled to free representation from a local Legal Services agency, under specific circumstances. As discussed in chapter 3, however, there are severe limitations upon such agencies' resources and their authority to pursue issues aggressively on behalf of the poor. In many other civil cases, poor people will simply be unable to pursue their claims, regardless of the strength of the claims, simply because the claimants lack the necessary resources to bring a case to court.

In the 1971 case of *Boddie v. Connecticut*, the Supreme Court ruled that states could not deny poor people access to courts for divorce proceedings because of inability to pay court costs.[26] The decision did not eliminate filing fees and court costs as a barrier to poor people in all civil cases because the Court based its reasoning upon the state's monopolization of the divorce process and the fundamental rights embodied in decisions about marriage and divorce. The ruling did not require fee waiver in any other types of civil cases. In concurring opinions, Justices William O. Douglas and William Brennan argued that the Court should eliminate discrimination against the poor by applying equal access to justice in all civil proceedings.

In subsequent cases, the Supreme Court demonstrated its lack of concern for equal access to civil courts. In *United States v. Kras*, the Court decided that an unemployed indigent, who was supporting his spouse, his mother, and three small children, including one with cystic fibrosis, could be barred from initiating bankruptcy proceedings because of his inability to pay the $50 filing fee.[27] In *Kras*, the four Nixon appointees plus Justice White sidestepped the apparent similarity between bankruptcy proceedings and the *Boddie* rationale about government monopolization of divorce. The majority further argued that the indigent petitioner should be able to pay the filing fee through an installment plan, a justification that had been rejected in

Boddie for divorce cases. As Justice Stewart noted wryly in his dissent, "some of the poor are too poor even to go bankrupt."[28] Justice Thurgood Marshall castigated the majority for basing its decision upon the assumption that desperately poor people could save enough money to pay a filing fee.

In a second case in which the four Nixon appointees were joined by Justice White, *Ortwein v. Schwab*, the Court determined that an inability to pay court filing fees could bar welfare recipients from seeking judicial review of administrative reductions in their benefits.[29] Thus, any errors or improprieties in a state agency's decision to reduce welfare could be immunized from judicial scrutiny and correction if the recipients were too poor to bring their cases to court. According to Justice Douglas, such wealth-based barriers to access to the courts create "a scheme of judicial review whereby justice remains a luxury for the wealthy."[30]

These decisions are indicative of the Supreme Court's acceptance of wealth discrimination as a factor determining who will have access to the resources and protections of the judicial branch of government. According to Gayle Binion, a scholar who has carefully studied Supreme Court decisions affecting the poor:

> The Supreme Court should be faulted for its decisions in [*Kras*] and [*Ortwein*], not only for its lack of candor in its attempts to differentiate [*Boddie*] and its hostility to the material interests of the poor, but as well for ignoring the central issue of access to judicial processes. Resolution of legal disputes is an inherently and uniquely governmental function; access to the courts is a fundamental right of citizenship. . . . [B]y deciding that inability to pay would bar access to the courts, [the Supreme Court] has decided that the law shall not protect those unable to pay.[31]

The development of the Supreme Court's view of the poor has been heavily influenced by the political factors which affect the Court's composition at any moment in history. In the decisions affecting right to counsel for indigent defendants and access to civil court processes, the appointments made by President Nixon steered the Court away from the Warren-era developments which advanced equal access to the Courts. Lucius and Twiley Barker have clearly illuminated the influence of appointments by comparing two cases decided just as the Nixon appointees joined the Court.[32] In the 1972 case of *Fuentes v. Shevin*, the Court ruled, four to three, that there must be a hearing before a state can order the seizure of a debtor's property upon application of a creditor.[33] This decision provided procedural protections for poor people being pursued by creditors. In a subsequent case involving the same Court members plus the addition of Nixon appointees Lewis Powell and William Rehnquist, the two newcomers joined the three *Fuentes* dissenters to permit seizure of debtors' property without notice to the debtor and *prior to* a hearing.[34] This decision endorsed a Louisiana statute clearly designed to advance the interests of creditors.

In a sharp dissenting opinion, Justice Stewart noted that "[t]he only perceivable change that has occurred since *Fuentes* is in the makeup of the Court."[35] Stewart further argued that:

> A basic change in the law upon a ground no firmer than a change in our membership invites the popular misconception that this institution is little different from the two political branches of the Government. No misconception could do more lasting injury to this Court and to the system of law which it is our abiding mission to serve.[36]

Although Stewart believed, or perhaps pretended to believe, that Supreme Court decisions and constitutional law are based entirely upon legal principles, his own argument reinforces the fact that judicial decisions are influenced by political forces (e.g., the election of a new president) which affect the Court's composition. This so-called "misconception" that political factors influence judicial decisions is, in fact, a harsh reality which detrimentally affects the interests of poor people who lack political power, access, and representation in all three branches of government.

Education

According to James Coleman, the concept of equal educational opportunity "has been implicit in most educational practice throughout most of the period of [American] public education in the nineteenth and twentieth centuries."[37] Although the American concept of equality has not meant absolute equality in availability of educational resources, it does represent a rejection of the class divisions within other countries' educational systems. In the American context, the concept of equal educational opportunity has led to a national policy of free public education for all children through high school.

Judicial decisions affect educational policies when individuals assert that their constitutional rights are infringed upon by policies implemented in local school districts. Some court cases affect mandatory religious practices and censorship, both of which implicate First Amendment rights, while other cases address claims of unconstitutional discrimination. There have been several significant deci-sions affecting educational opportunities for poor children based on asserted constitutional violations of the Equal Protection Clause.

School Financing

The initial cases affecting educational opportunities for the poor resulted in judicial approval of financing schemes which re-quired the entire public, whether parents or not, to pay taxes to sup-port public education. For example, in a Michigan court case in 1874, the famous jurist Thomas Cooley declared that education was "re-garded as an important practical advantage to be supplied . . . to rich and poor alike, and not something . . . to be brought as such within the reach of those whose accumulated wealth enabled them to pay for it."[38] Thus, education was viewed as both a responsibility of govern-ment and as an essential building block for individuals' opportunities and success in American society.

The seminal Supreme Court case affecting poor schoolchildren was *San Antonio Independent School District v. Rodriguez* in 1973.[39] The case arose because, as in other states, the Texas system of financ-ing local schools through property taxes created gross disparities in the educational resources available to children in various districts throughout the state. In the Edgewood Independent School District, for instance, the district's $1.05 tax rate per $100 of assessed property value generated only $26 per pupil per year. By contrast, because of higher property values in the more affluent neighboring school dis-trict of Alamo Heights, a lower property tax rate of $.85 generated $333 per pupil. The state's educational programs exacerbated this dis-parity by providing more money per pupil to the wealthier district. Federal aid to education made a modest reduction in the disparity by providing more aid to the poorer district, so that the final total was a significant disparity of $356 per pupil available in Edgewood and $594 per pupil in Alamo Heights. As a result of the disparity, novice teach-ers used Edgewood to gain experience before quickly moving to higher paying districts. The students in Edgewood were taught by many teachers who could not qualify for state certification and who were permitted to work in classrooms temporarily with emergency teaching permits. By contrast, the more highly trained, experienced teachers in Alamo Heights fulfilled state certification requirements and nearly 40 percent of them possessed advanced educational de-grees. Each of the school counselors in Edgewood had to help six times as many students as their counterparts in Alamo Heights.[40]

In a five to four decision, with all four Nixon appointees in the majority, the Court determined that there is no fundamental right to education and that economic status is not a suspect classification under the Equal Protection Clause. The majority claimed that any remedy for this harmful inequality must come from elected officials in state legislatures, despite the fact that legislators, like others with political power in the United States, represent, and are themselves, affluent middle-class individuals who benefit from the disparities in school financing. In deferring to the other branches of government, the Court majority ignored the harmful effects upon politically powerless poor people. Thus, Texas and other states could retain their school financing systems despite the obvious disparities and adverse impacts upon the poor. As a result, poor children, who frequently have the greatest need for additional educational resources, can fall farther behind affluent children in securing opportunities for success in American society.

In a famous dissenting opinion, Justice Thurgood Marshall complained that "the right of every American to an equal start in life, so far as the provision of a state service as important as education is concerned, is far too vital to permit state discrimination."[41]

In considering the policy-making powers of courts, the Supreme Court's decision is understandable not only in terms of the majority's insensitivity to wealth discrimination, but also in its reluctance to initiate such a far-reaching, controversial reform. A decision against inequality would have required sweeping school finance reforms throughout the country and would have resulted in school boards losing some of their traditional control over local schools. Supreme Court decisions are not self-executing, so the justices, or at least some justices, may fear that judicial policy decisions in public education will generate significant political opposition and resistance. As Robert Bennett has observed:

> Two of the major contributions of the Warren Court to constitutional jurisprudence—the school desegregation and legislative apportionment decisions—required a willingness to devote extraordinary judicial resources to a continuing process of overseeing the responsive actions of other branches of government. In [*San Antonio Independent School District v. Rodriguez*] the Court may well have thought that attacking the school financing problem would have required just such an extraordinary devotion of resources; that prospect could have chilled the enthusiasm of a Court quite appalled by unequal educational financing.[42]

In the aftermath of the *San Antonio* case, efforts were made to obtain legislative relief for inequality in educational funding. As one scholar has noted, however, such efforts collided with "the reality of the legislatures' inability and unwillingness to squarely address" this school financing issue.[43] The vacuum created by legislative indifference and Supreme Court abdication has slowly been filled by state judges. In the years following the *San Antonio* decision, several state courts have declared that education is a protected right and have ordered state governments to redress wealth discrimination problems in school financing.

In the mid-1970s, state supreme courts in California and New Jersey broke new ground by ordering equalization in school financing.[44] These decisions and several others have recognized educational rights for poor people through state constitutional provisions over which state supreme courts, rather than the U.S. Supreme Court, are the ultimate authorities. According to one study, even unsuccessful cases, such as *San Antonio*, result in some modest improvements toward equalization by pushing equal educational opportunity onto the agendas of other policy makers, such as state courts and legislatures.[45]

The disparities among Texas school districts continued to grow after the 1973 decision. By 1988, the $238-per-pupil disparity between Edgewood and Alamo Heights at the time of the *San Antonio* case had grown to a whopping $1,300 per pupil per year.[46] In 1989, when the disparity between Edgewood and the wealthiest districts elsewhere in the state had reached as much as $8,400 per pupil per year, the Texas Supreme Court intervened and struck down the state's school financing system.[47]

Although only a few state courts have entered the educational policy fray by ordering legislatures to create financing equalization measures, there appears to be a growing movement toward examining school financing issues. These policy changes are not necessarily the result of any heightened societal concern about discrimination against the poor. Rather, the appearance of cases challenging unequal school financing in several states coincides with increasing attention by political actors and policymakers everywhere to weaknesses in the entire country's educational system. Thus far, the policy changes which lessen resource discrimination against the poor have been initiated by the judicial branch, albeit generally from state courts rather than the symbolic leaders of the judiciary, namely, the justices of the United States Supreme Court.

Although several state supreme courts have invalidated school financing systems that create severe inequalities, these judicial decisions have not automatically led to policies that equalize educational resources. Judges have a limited ability to implement their policy decisions, so they generally are dependent upon legislatures and executive branch officials obeying judicial policy directives. As a result, school financing cases can lead to significant symbolic decisions that place school financing on a state's policy agenda without necessarily achieving the level of equalization envisioned by the judge. A study of the California Supreme Court's equalization case indicates that the actual progress toward changing the financing system depended upon legislative responses to the court's decision. The study's author concluded that:

> School reform advocates sought change in the courts primarily because they lacked the political power to move the legislature. However, the courts do not necessarily possess the leverage to secure action from a recalcitrant legislature. Courts must depend upon a close correspondence of interest from legislators if favorable action is to be achieved.[48]

Access to Education

In 1982, the U.S. Supreme Court struck down a Texas statute that barred illegal aliens from the public schools. In a five to four decision in *Plyler v. Doe*, opposed by three members of the *San Antonio* majority plus a Reagan appointee, the majority granted illegal aliens the full protection of the Equal Protection Clause by applying strict scrutiny analysis to the statute.[49] In the Court's opinion, Justice Brennan emphasized the importance of educational opportunities for children in American society:

> [The Texas law] imposes a lifetime hardship on a discrete class of children not accountable for their disabling status. The stigma of illiteracy will mark them for the rest of their lives. By denying these children a basic education, we deny them the ability to live within the structure of our civic institutions, and foreclose any realistic possibility that they will contribute in even the smallest way to the progress of our Nation.[50]

If the Court had applied the same words and legal analysis in the *San Antonio* case, the state's discriminatory school financing system would have been declared unconstitutional. In the *San Antonio* case, even the State of Texas admitted that its financing system would be clearly invalid if the Court chose to apply the Equal Protection Clause for the benefit of less affluent students. The Court majority in 1973, however, decided that the Equal Protection Clause did not apply to the poor, despite the harms they may suffer from a discriminatory school financing system. Why did illegal alien children, recognized by the Court as poor and "special members of this underclass,"[51] receive the benefit of more demanding Equal Protection analysis than that applied for homegrown poor children in the *San Antonio* case?

Based upon their dissents in *San Antonio*, Justices Brennan and Marshall clearly believe that both groups should benefit from the Equal Protection Clause to eliminate discrimination in education. Justice John Paul Stevens, who was appointed after the *San Antonio* decision, joined the Brennan opinion on illegal alien children and may share the same views regarding all poor children. The remaining two members of the majority in the *Plyler* case, Justices Lewis Powell and Harry Blackmun, believed that the two cases were distinguishable. One basis for distinguishing the cases, as discussed in chapter 5, is the fact that the Court had previously protected aliens with strict Equal Protection analysis in a few cases but had never explicitly declared that wealth discrimination received similar constitutional attention. This possible distinction, however, does not underlie the justifications advanced by Powell and Blackmun for supporting access to education in one context but rejecting equal educational opportunity in another.

Justice Powell, whose *San Antonio* majority opinion stated that "the ultimate solutions must come from the lawmakers and from the democratic pressures of those who elect them,"[52] seemed to have lost faith in the effective policy-making abilities of other branches of government. Although the *Plyler* dissenters admitted that it was "folly" and "wrong" to bar alien children from public schools, they evinced a deference to other branches of government consistent with the majority opinion in *San Antonio*.[53] If the elected state officials wished to pursue this damaging, discriminatory policy, then the *Plyler* dissenters felt that the judiciary should not interfere. Powell, on the other hand, broke ranks and noted that "Congress has not provided effective leadership with [the illegal immigration] problem" and therefore illegal alien "children should not be left on the streets uneducated."[54] Although the same rationale could have been applied to legislative inaction on school financing policies that harm children in less affluent districts, perhaps Powell was deterred by the more far-reaching policy consequences of such an intrusive decision in the *San Antonio* case.

By contrast, Justice Blackmun drew a distinction between a complete deprivation of education for illegal alien children and merely inferior education for poor children in *San Antonio*. However, as with Powell's concurring opinion, Blackmun's justifications for distinguishing the two cases by emphasizing the role of education in society could easily be applied to all poor children. Justice Blackmun asserted that a complete denial of education "strike[s] at the very heart of equal protection values by involving the State in the creation of permanent class distinctions."[55] It seems apparent, although Blackmun did not acknowledge it, that the grossly inferior educational resources and opportunities provided to poor American children through inequitable school financing systems can contribute to precisely the same undesirable result.

School Desegregation and Educational Opportunity for the Poor

The federal courts' school desegregation decisions that emanated from *Brown v. Board of Education* and its progeny focused upon the elimination of unconstitutional racial discrimination in education. Because of the relationship between race and economic status in American society, these decisions inevitably influenced educational opportunities for poor children. School desegregation orders served to equalize opportunities across socioeconomic as well as racial lines in heterogeneous cities in which poor African-American children were crowded into inferior, segregated schools. This effect was particularly evident in medium-size cities without substantial suburban concentrations of affluent people and in countywide school systems comprised of the entire socioeconomic spectrum of society.

A school desegregation decision by the Supreme Court in 1974 served not only to halt the development of further judicial remedies for racial segregation, but also to exacerbate the inequalities in educational opportunities affecting poor children in large cities. In *Milliken v. Bradley*, the Supreme Court rejected a lower court order requiring that the students in segregated Detroit schools be mixed with students in dozens of suburban school districts in order to achieve desegregation.[56] Despite evidence of the State of Michigan's contributions to school segregation in Detroit and a history of government programs fostering housing discrimination between cities and suburbs, the Court decided that remedies must be limited to single school districts unless there is specific proof of suburban districts' direct participation in engendering segregation. The Court handicapped any potential remedies by refusing to recognize that metropolitan segregation was the result of historical forces involving the participation and acquiescence of many actors beyond the narrow boundaries of central city school districts.

By limiting desegregation orders within individual districts, the decision in *Milliken v. Bradley* effectively guaranteed that districts containing significant majorities of poor, minority students would remain segregated. As a result, schools only a few blocks apart may be entirely different—poor and minority versus affluent and white—by virtue of being on opposite sides of some invisible and often relatively arbitrary dividing line between school districts within the same metropolitan area.

This five to four decision in *Milliken*, which, like *San Antonio*, is frequently attributed to the majority's reluctance to tackle a controversial policy issue despite strong evidence and a constitutional basis for doing so, severely restricted one avenue for increasing educational equality for poor students in urban areas.

In larger metropolitan areas, the concentrations of poor people within the cities and affluent people in the suburbs can contribute to differing educational resources, especially in property tax financing systems that adversely affect older cities with declining tax bases. Gary Orfield's study of metropolitan desegregation efforts has documented the burdens placed upon less affluent people by the existence of a plethora of separate, locally controlled school districts around large cities.[57] Even if an income tax financing system were implemented, the cities containing poorer citizens would generate fewer dollars per pupil. Although cities and suburbs frequently share other public services such as regional public transportation, water, power, and other services, the Supreme Court's decision in *Milliken* helped to rigidify separate educational systems within metropolitan areas. Thus, the well-documented declines in many urban school systems narrow the prospects of poor students while affluent students a few miles away reap significant educational advantages. The ongoing developments toward greater equalization of educational financing should reduce these disparities, but these changes have impacted only a few states thus far.

Housing

Except for the Third Amendment provision against quartering soldiers in a private home without the owner's permission, the Constitution makes no reference to housing. For poor people, access to housing is dependent upon market forces, including their own financial resources, the available supply of affordable housing, and government programs that provide housing assistance and public housing. In a 1972 case challenging an Oregon statute favoring landlords in legal proceedings related to evictions, the Supreme Court clearly rejected any notion that a right to housing could be found in the Constitution.[58] Although the Supreme Court has developed constitutional rights, such as privacy, which are not explicitly mentioned in the Constitution, the Supreme Court has declined to recognize any constitutional right to housing. Justice White declared for the Court:

We do not denigrate the importance of decent, safe, and sanitary housing. But the Constitution does not provide judicial remedies for every
social and economic ill. We are unable to perceive in that document
any constitutional guarantee of access to dwellings of a particular quality, . . . Absent constitutional mandate, the assurance of adequate
housing and the definition of landlord-tenant relationships are legislative, not judicial, functions.[59]

The Court's reluctance to consider the existence of a right to
housing is understandable when considered in light of the significant
expense upon government that would accompany such a judicial policy. Unlike education, in which the structures for providing services
for all children are already in place and would merely have to be
equalized if education were a recognized right, a right to housing
would be extremely expensive to implement. Although the courts
have not guaranteed access to housing for poor people, there have
been many important judicial decisions addressing racial discrimination in the provision of housing. These decisions have had important
consequences for the availability of housing for the poor.

Zoning Practices and the Poor

Communities frequently use zoning requirements to define the
character of buildings and lots that are permitted within a jurisdiction.
Because zoning requirements in many desirable residential communities demand large lots and expensive single-family dwellings, poor people can be effectively precluded from buying or renting housing. These
practices have frequently been challenged on grounds of racial and
wealth discrimination. The decisions of the Supreme Court on zoning
matters have limited poor people's prospects for gaining opportunities
to move out of declining urban areas and into more affluent suburbs
that contain better schools and other social services.

In *James v. Valtierra*, a 1971 case challenging a provision of the
California constitution, the Supreme Court approved a state constitutional amendment requiring voter approval for any low-income housing projects within a community.[60] A previous case had rejected an Akron, Ohio city charter provision permitting voter-controlled housing
discrimination.[61] The five-member Court majority in *James* distinguished the two cases by noting that the Akron ordinance was impermissible because it encouraged racial discrimination through its al-
lowance of a veto over fair housing ordinances. In effect, then, the
Supreme Court rejected laws evincing racial discrimination as a motivation but accepted overt majoritarian control over the housing oppor-

tunities of the minority of citizens who live in poverty. In many metropolitan areas, this ability to exclude poor people has racial as well as wealth discrimination effects.

In subsequent cases, the Court erected barriers to lawsuits challenging discriminatory zoning practices and, in the words of Barker and Barker, "made it clear that the invocation of [zoning and land use] powers to block the construction of low-income housing does not offend the [C]onstitution."[62] In *Warth v. Seldin*, the four Nixon appointees formed the core of a five-member majority that said that individuals and public interest organizations could not sue a suburb over zoning practices that excluded low- and moderate-income housing.[63] One scholar has remarked that the plaintiffs in *Warth* were placed in a "legal 'Catch-22.' "[64] They were not permitted to sue because they did not own property in the suburb and therefore were supposedly not directly affected by the challenged zoning laws. Because the zoning laws operated to prevent them from buying affordable property, they had little hope of ever acquiring property in order to meet the Supreme Court's threshold requirement for filing suit against those laws.

In two subsequent cases, real estate developers acquired property and then sought to gain zoning changes that would permit construction of low- and moderate-income housing. Thus, they followed the Supreme Court's requirements in *Warth* for demonstrating a sufficient interest, namely, property ownership, for filing suit. In one case, a city emulated the California constitutional provision in *James* by creating a city-charter provision requiring voter approval for a zoning change.[65] In the other case, the Supreme Court rejected the challenge to exclusionary zoning practices by requiring plaintiffs to bear the significant burden of proving that racial discriminatory intent underlay the zoning decisions.[66] The effect of these decisions is to permit exclusionary zoning practices that limit the availability of affordable housing for poor people and that frequently confine less affluent people to declining urban centers. As Gayle Binion has argued, when the Supreme Court's zoning decisions are added to its education decisions affecting the poor, less affluent people are precluded from gaining access to governmental resources equivalent to those available to middle-class and wealthy citizens:

> The Court's decisions in the property/housing cases and its decision in
> *San Antonio Independent School District v. Rodriguez* . . . serve to mutually reinforce the isolation of the disadvantaged. . . . Control over
> zoning by local governments prevents the poor from becoming residents of particular communities; it similarly denies them access to resources, especially educational, that are potentially available.[67]

Housing Discrimination

The Supreme Court's inaction in the face of housing discrimination against the poor can be attributed to its narrow view that the Equal Protection Clause does not prevent wealth discrimination and to its reluctance to intervene in a potentially far-reaching, controversial policy area. Some court decisions, on the other hand, have increased opportunities for poor people through enforcement of laws against racial discrimination in housing.

Phillip Cooper's case study of housing discrimination litigation affecting Parma, Ohio, illustrates the limitations of judicial policy directives.[68] The U.S. Justice Department challenged Parma's efforts to exclude low-income and public housing projects as a violation of the Fair Housing Act. There was substantial evidence of racially discriminatory motives because several city officials said openly at public meetings that they did not want African-Americans moving into Parma.

The judicial process operated at its usual slow pace. The discriminatory actions by the city of Parma occurred from 1968 to 1972. The Justice Department initiated legal action in 1973 but the case did not come to trial until late in 1979. The federal district judge found in mid-1980 that Parma had engaged in illegal housing discrimination and he ordered the city to begin working with the Department of Justice to develop a remedy. The city refused to cooperate and it unsuccessfully pursued appeals all the way to the Supreme Court, which declined to hear the case in 1982. No remedial efforts were initiated until fourteen years after Parma's discriminatory polices were first questioned.

The district court made a committee of Parma citizens responsible for developing the details of a remedy. They initiated efforts to develop a public housing agency, apply for construction funds, cooperate with regional housing authorities, and advertise Parma as a city open to racial minorities. However, by the time Parma began working to rectify its housing discrimination problem in the mid-1980s, federal funds for low-income housing had dried up. In the mid-1970s, Parma had the opportunity to obtain millions of dollars through the federal Community Development Block Grant program but lost the money when it refused to apply any of the funds to low-income housing. Although judicial pressures had forced the city to change its discriminatory housing policies in the 1980s, low-income people gained few benefits because there were no longer funds available to build affordable housing. Parma finally built a sixty-unit public housing project in 1987; but in a city of 92,000 people, one modest project does not amount to much of an increase in the availability of housing for less affluent people. The Parma housing case, which "[l]egal experts and civil rights advocates considered the most comprehensive fair housing opinion ever written,"[69] has yielded only slow, minimal changes for the benefit of poor people. In sum, the Parma case illustrates how ponderous and ineffective judicial policy making can be, even when a court acts to remedy illegal actions that disadvantage less affluent people.

Welfare Benefits

Supreme Court decisions regarding welfare benefits have reflected, according to one scholar, "a deep-seated ambivalence" stemming from internal disputes over whether such entitlements should be viewed as rights or merely as privileges.[70] Presumably, if the poor have a *right* to welfare benefits and a governmental action impinges upon that protected right, judges should apply strict scrutiny in forcing the government to present a compelling justification for its actions. If, however, welfare benefits are only a privilege, then a court should be more deferential to governmental actions affecting those benefits.

In the 1969 case of *Shapiro v. Thompson*, the Supreme Court applied strict scrutiny in striking down a state law mandating a one-year residency requirement for welfare eligibility.[71] Because the statute interfered with citizens' fundamental right to travel, the Court rejected several rational justifications for the law, including reduced burdens on scarce state resources and preservation of available funds for deserving state taxpayers. The Court did not recognize any of the justifications for the state law as compelling. The following year the decision in *Goldberg v. Kelly* built upon this judicially protective approach to welfare entitlements by declaring that states must provide evidentiary hearings prior to termination of public assistance payments.[72] In the majority opinion, Justice Brennan declared that a welfare termination decision "involves state action that adjudicates important *rights*" (emphasis added) and rejected an assertion that benefits are merely a privilege.[73] In fact, Brennan even adopted a scholarly argument, popular during the early 1970s, that welfare entitlements should be regarded as property. In Brennan's words, "[I]t may be realistic today to regard welfare entitlements as more like 'property' than a 'gratuity.' "[74] Subsequent decisions indicated, however, that Brennan's powerfully stated views on welfare benefits did not enjoy support among his colleagues, especially as the composition of the Court began to change with the addition of President Nixon's appointees.

For example, within weeks after establishing procedural protections for welfare recipients and despite objections from Brennan and two other justices, a different majority placed limits upon the Court's willingness to scrutinize state welfare laws. In *Dandridge v. Williams*, the Court upheld a Maryland statute which generally provided benefits according to need and family size but which detrimentally affected large families by creating a maximum monthly payment of $250.[75] In the Court's opinion, Justice Stewart declared that welfare benefits should not be regarded as rights deserving close scrutiny and protection by the judiciary: "[H]ere we deal with state regulation in the social and economic field, not affecting freedoms guaranteed by the Bill of Rights, and claimed to violate the Fourteenth Amendment only because . . . [of] some disparity in grants of welfare payments to the largest AFDC families."[76]

As the composition of the Supreme Court changed during the 1970s, the majority followed the *Dandridge* model of treating welfare benefits as privileges which could be affected by laws for merely rational rather than compelling reasons. For example, the Court approved mandatory visits to welfare recipients' homes by caseworkers despite dissenters' concerns about providing less judicial protection against unreasonable searches to poor people than that provided to other citizens and even to businesses.[77] The majority presumed, in a paternalistic manner, that caseworkers help recipients rather than seek to oversee or to interfere with recipients' personal lives. In so doing, the majority defined poor people's rights differently from those of other citizens. As Justice Marshall indicated in his dissent, if such intrusions were visited upon more affluent Americans, such as having IRS agents make mandatory visits to all taxpayers' homes to document the number of dependents, the Court would view them as an invasion of citizens' personal lives. Justice Marshall concluded that if an IRS law imposed a similar burden upon other citizens, "the cries of constitutional outrage would be unanimous."[78]

Although the Court decided several cases that approved discriminatory and otherwise detrimental statutes affecting welfare recipients during the 1970s and 1980s, the Court's continuing ambivalence about the precise status of welfare benefits remained evident. In a 1979 decision rejecting a gender-based statute which discriminated against unemployed mothers, Justice Blackmun's majority opinion rejected "a return to the discredited view that welfare benefits are a 'privilege' not subject to the guarantee of equal protection."[79] This apparent ambivalence about the protection to be afforded welfare beneficiaries has not manifested itself in opinions returning to the strict scrutiny standard applied in *Shapiro* and *Goldberg*. In fact,

John Brigham's research on the Court's approach to protection of property in the era of Chief Justice Rehnquist during the late 1980s indicates a movement away from protecting welfare benefits as property or as vested rights, even as the Court majority provides greater protection for traditional forms of property, such as real estate, owned by more affluent people.[80]

The Poor as Invisible Pawns in Policy Debates

The judiciary becomes involved in many policy issues that do not focus directly upon the poor. As the policy battles over abortion demonstrate, however, the poor can suffer the harshest consequences from policy-making decisions ostensibly aimed at issues that are assumed to be separate from the problems of wealth discrimination and poverty.

The Supreme Court's 1973 decision in *Roe v. Wade* limited the ability of state governments to restrict women's choices regarding abortion.[81] Because choices about abortion were recognized as a component of the established constitutional right to privacy, states could not ban abortions during the first six months of pregnancy. The controversial decision mobilized anti-abortion interest groups and led to congressional and state legislation to restrict the availability of public funding for abortions.[82] When these restrictions specifically aimed at limiting poor women's options for choosing abortion were challenged in court, the Supreme Court upheld the legislative restrictions. In *Maher v. Roe*, for example, the Court approved Connecticut's practice of paying the childbirth expenses of indigent women but refusing to fund nontherapeutic abortions.[83] The Court not only followed its usual course in declining to apply the Equal Protection Clause to forbid this obvious wealth discrimination, but they also sidestepped *Roe*'s reasoning that characterized the abortion choice as a component of the fundamental right to privacy. As Justice Brennan noted in a dissenting opinion:

> This disparity in funding by the State clearly operates to coerce indigent women to bear children they would not otherwise choose to have, and just as clearly, this coercion can only operate upon the poor, who are uniquely the victims of this form of financial pressure.[84]

In the eyes of most observers, President Reagan's appointment of Justice Anthony Kennedy in 1988 apparently tipped the delicate balance on the Court toward changing previous decisions upholding abortion. In the 1989 case of *Webster v. Reproductive Health Ser-*

vices, a new majority on the Court approved greater state restrictions upon access to abortion by upholding legislation forbidding abortions in public hospitals and by requiring viability testing by doctors prior to abortions.[85] Four of the justices were clearly inclined to overturn *Roe v. Wade,* but were waiting (and hoping) for Justice Sandra O'Connor to supply the needed fifth vote in some future case directly challenging the 1973 precedent. The decision served as an invitation for state legislatures to pass restrictive laws, especially those limiting poor women's access to public medical facilities.

Many anti-abortion activists were excited about the prospects for a new direction in Supreme Court decisions on abortion. However, a practical examination of the abortion issue reveals that no matter what the Court ultimately decides about *Roe v. Wade,* abortions will continue to be legal and available in many places throughout the United States. The only foreseeable impact is that poor women will be denied the choice that more affluent women will continue to enjoy.

Political analysts in 1989 predicted that ten states would clearly keep abortion available as a choice for women and twenty-two others might keep it available depending upon political battles within their legislatures.[86] The continued availability of abortion in some states but not in others simply means that affluent women will have to travel elsewhere for abortions if such procedures are restricted in their home states. Thus, only poor women within restrictive states will be deprived of the opportunity to have abortions. In essence, the new Court majority's apparent inclination to place the abortion issue back in the hands of elected state legislatures will merely exacerbate discriminatory consequences for poor women rather than settle the nation's divisive and irresoluble policy debate about the issue.

Judicial Policy Making and the Poor

Courts have avoided recognizing poor people as a discrete, victimized class of citizens and thereby have failed to provide them with the legal protections granted to other political minorities. The poor are ignored, in part, because of a general insensitivity to wealth discrimination prevalent in American society. Moreover, judges may have very practical reasons for their reluctance to address wealth discrimination because of the potential difficulties in implementing remedial orders. Judicial orders addressing wealth discrimination in education, housing, or some other policy areas may have far-reaching consequences which would require state and local governments to expend significant resources in order to facilitate equal opportunity.

The poor lack visibility and political influence in legislative bodies so judges can have no confidence that legislatures will be motivated to cooperate in altering discriminatory policies.

In sum, contrary to the Supreme Court's visible slogan of "Equal Justice Under Law," the judiciary has demonstrated little sensitivity or concern about the detrimental impact of discriminatory policies upon poor people. However, even if judges were interested in redressing obvious inequalities, the limited effectiveness of judicial policy-making constrains any potential efforts to use court decisions to address fundamental problems of wealth discrimination and economic inequality.

CHAPTER SEVEN

Courts and the Poor in Comparative Contexts

Although various countries possess differing legal systems and court structures, many espouse the common goal of treating citizens equally within their judicial processes. The degree to which this goal is genuinely pursued depends upon the structure of government, the distribution of political power, and the predominant social values within each country. A comparative examination of judicial systems in other countries can illuminate the influential elements and processes underlying the American courts and perhaps can provide examples of potentially valuable reforms.

Constitutions and Judicial Authority

One important difference between the American judicial system and courts in other countries involves the power of the judiciary within the governing system. Because judges in the United States possess significant authority under the American constitutional system, they differ from judges in most other countries in their ability to influence judicial outcomes and public policy through their personal judgments.

The blueprint for the structure of the American national government is the U.S. Constitution. The Constitution is a relatively brief document which describes the three branches of government (i.e., legislative, executive, and judicial), generally establishes the branches' respective spheres of authority, and specifies the rights possessed by individual citizens that cannot be infringed by the government. Many countries throughout the world also utilize national constitutions to design their governing systems. Although some constitutions emulate the United States constitution, other countries' fundamental charters contain many provisions different from those in the American document.

For example, according to J. Woodford Howard, social constitutions are popular in the Third World.[1] These constitutions contain a multitude of guarantees of economic rights and social services to be provided by the government. In other words, they contain detailed descriptions of government policies and programs. The Nigerian constitution, for example, declares that the government has a duty to encourage intermarriage between people of different ethnic and religious groups in order to foster national integration and unity.[2] These detailed constitutional provisions frequently differ from the general provisions of the United States Constitution which leave specific programs and policies to be developed through legislation. Detailed constitutions create greater clarity about the meaning of constitutional provisions but thereby force a corresponding reduction in the power of judges to interpret and define those provisions. Because of their broad coverage, social constitutions create risks that a government will not be able to accomplish all of its stated goals. According to Howard, "The greater danger in maximalist, social constitutions is this: If too many promises go unfulfilled, will the people lose faith in constitutionalism itself?"[3]

The Soviet Union provides a striking example of a constitutionally based system of government that differs dramatically from the American constitutional system. The constitution of the Soviet Union contains many guarantees for its citizens. There are guarantees that emphasize the Soviet goal of equality of condition among citizens, including rights to medical care, housing, and education.[4] The constitution also guarantees personal rights of freedom of speech and exercise of religion. The right to freedom of conscience explicitly protects religious beliefs and practices, and the right to lodge a complaint about a public official's actions provides protection for a specific category of expression.[5] As these Soviet examples illustrate, the existence of specific guarantees in a written constitution does not ensure that people actually enjoy legal protections. Many dissidents in the Soviet Union have been imprisoned for criticizing the government or for attempting to practice their religion. The contradiction between the stated constitutional protections and the actual repressive practices reflects the limited role of law and the judiciary in the Soviet Union's government system, as well as a political ideology that limits individual freedom.

Courts in the Soviet Union do not possess the power to overrule the other branches of government. Judges in the Soviet Union are very weak in comparison with the leaders of the Communist party and heads of government departments. By contrast, the power of judicial review in the United States, although not specified in the Constitution, has been practiced by the Supreme Court and accepted as a component of the governing system since 1803.[6] Judicial review, namely, the power of judges to declare acts of the legislature and executive to be unconstitutional, has made the judiciary a co-equal branch in the American governing system and has served as the basis for protecting individuals' rights and for initiating judicial policy-making.

Because Soviet judges exercise little authority within the governing system, actual power resides in other governmental actors. The discretionary authority wielded by government officials is much more important than the words written in the Soviet constitution. As Louise Shelley found in her study of Soviet lawyers, "Because [government officials] do not feel obliged to adhere to codified law and legal regulations, Soviet officials have more latitude in their decision making, increasing their power over the populace."[7] Thus, the weakness of formal law in the Soviet Union results from the concentration of political power in the Communist Party and central government and the dearth of effective power allocated to the judiciary. In fact, the Soviet system intentionally limits the potential power of judges by explicitly granting to the Presidium, the thirty-nine member legislative body elected from the Supreme Soviet, the ultimate power to oversee interpretation and enforcement of the constitution.[8]

Governing systems with weak judiciaries are not limited to communist systems. Many democratic governments have weak judicial branches. Parliament's power in Great Britain cannot be checked by any supreme judicial court and the French Constitutional Council has very limited powers in relation to a powerful executive branch.[9] Even in Canada, which has a Charter of Rights and Freedoms as well as a power of judicial review, Parliament has the authority to suspend major individual rights for five years.[10] Because political power under these constitutional governing systems is concentrated outside the courts, these judiciaries have little ability to initiate public policies or to expand individuals' constitutional rights.

By contrast, judges in the United States possess significant power. In the American federal courts, this power is enhanced by the life tenure and protected salaries of judges, which permit independent decision making. Job security alone, however, does not create strong judicial power, as evidenced by the life-tenured British judges whose authority is narrower than their American counterparts.

Broad American judicial power derives from the nature of the United States Constitution. The Constitution's limited specificity is considered one of its greatest strengths because the governing system can adapt to changing social circumstances. In the words of Archibald Cox:

[T]he genius of the Framers was partly a talent for saying enough but not too much. . . . [I]mportant questions were left open, questions that the Framers could not foresee and questions on which they could not agree. [The Framers] left those questions to be decided as they came to a head in accordance with the dominant needs of each generation.[11]

Thus, judicial interpretations of the Constitution change throughout history in accordance with societal changes and the political orientations of judges within a given era.

This constitutional flexibility, when coupled with the power of judicial review, gives the American judiciary significant authority within the governing system. Judicial officers can identify constitutional rights of individuals, including rights that are not expressly contained in the Bill of Rights, and can countermand actions by the legislative and executive branches that clash with the judges' interpretations of the Constitution. Judges in other countries cannot mandate public policies in opposition to the preferences of the ruling political authorities. American judges, however, possess the formal authority, if not always the inclination or the will, to protect poor people and other political minorities through judicial decisions that enforce the concept of equality within the Constitution. Thus, in contrast with other court systems, the American judiciary is a more active participant in policy developments that affect less affluent people.

An additional factor that enhances the influence of judges in the United States is the American adherence to a common-law system. The United States adopted the British legal system's practice of permitting judges to make new law through decisions in court cases. New judicial decisions presumably build upon previous decisions to create precedents that will guide judges in future cases. The judge's published opinion in each court case explains the reasoning underlying the judicial outcome, including new interpretations of law, if any. By contrast, in civil-law countries such as France and West Germany, legal codes are written by legislative bodies, and judges merely apply the detailed codes to decide cases. Although judges have influence over outcomes in both systems through their power to interpret and apply the law, the common-law system grants much greater power to judges through its conscious endorsement of judge-made law. Because American judges can build or alter legal rules through their decisions, they have greater direct power than do judges in civil-law countries over the judicial outcomes which affect individual litigants, including poor people. Thus judges' attitudes, values, and experiences which guide judicial decision making are especially influential in the United States because of the American judges' greater policy-making authority and their explicit authority to develop case law.

In sum, the common-law system, a flexible constitution, and the power of judicial review serve to empower judges with significant authority within the American governing system. Although policies affecting less affluent people in other countries depend almost exclusively upon the actions of legislative and executive actors, judges in the United States possess significant power to determine both individual judicial outcomes and larger public policies affecting poor people. Because American judges generally share the same dominant values and attitudes possessed by other influential political elites, however, the judiciary has given scant attention to issues of wealth discrimination despite its authority to initiate remedial policies.

Differences in Legal Systems

An important factor that differentiates the judicial process in the United States from legal systems in other countries is the American reliance upon courts for protecting individual rights and for initiating public policies. American are acutely aware of the fact that they possess "rights" that can be protected through formal legal proceedings. American society's emphasis on individualism and private property leads people to pursue disputes in order to seek vindication of their personal interests. In addition, the myriad conflicts between strangers in a commercialized, heterogeneous mass society, ranging from auto accidents on a city street to disputes between mail-order businesses and their customers, generate a need for courts to provide formal dispute-processing mechanisms. The extent of Americans' reliance upon courts as the forum for resolving perceived wrongs within society has led to characterizations of the United States as a "litigious society" in which citizens will file lawsuits over any dispute, whether significant or trivial. This growing utilization of law and the courts reflects changes in American legal culture as citizens increasingly expect that every perceived injury in society should be remedied by the law. Thus, Lawrence Friedman characterizes Americans as expecting "total justice" from the legal system.[12]

By contrast, the legal cultures and judicial structures in other countries lead to different expectations about courts and to alternative approaches to dispute processing. For example, Japan has a highly industrialized and commercialized society which should generate many disputes between citizens through their business and other relationships. Despite being a fertile environment for disputes,

Japan has very few lawyers and judges and relatively little litigation. Although the United States has 1 lawyer for every 360 people, Japan only has 1 lawyer for every 10,000 people.[13] Some scholars theorize that these lower litigation rates represent a difference in legal culture. In other words, Japan is a homogenous society in which people traditionally emphasize harmony, obedience, and cooperation. Within Japanese society an apology process serves an important function for concluding disputes without engaging in costly, time-consuming administrative or court proceedings.[14] Thus, instead of pursuing disputes, people behave in a conciliatory manner.[15]

An alternative theory, which has gained widespread acceptance among scholars, is that the Japanese intentionally created small judicial institutions in order to force people to process their disputes through alternative mechanisms.[16] For example, even though proportionally more law students take judicial exams in Japan than take bar exams in the United States, only 1.7 percent pass the Japanese exam while over 70 percent pass the American exam.[17] Thus the authorities deliberately limit the size of the legal profession by making the threshold examination inordinately difficult. As described by Marc Galanter, "the low rate of litigation in Japan evidences not the preferences of the population, but deliberate policy choices by political elites."[18] As a result, most disputes must go to less formal mediation services, such as the Japanese Civil Liberties Bureau.[19]

Does a constricted legal process and an emphasis on mediation lead to greater equality in judicial outcomes for the less affluent? In Japan, the emphasis on mediation does not prevent unequal justice. Discriminatory effects according to wealth and status are clearly discernible. People who lack resources and status are likely to experience less favorable outcomes in pursuing disputes in the Japanese system. A study in Tokyo that included cases in both litigation and mediation found that obtaining an attorney or legal specialist increased the likelihood of prevailing in disputes over automobile accidents and housing.[20] In Japan, however, it is difficult for less affluent people to obtain legal representation. Attorneys usually represent repeat users of legal specialists, such as professional landlords, or people who have connections with legal specialists through their business or professional contacts. According to one scholar, "Even when one is able to retain legal representation, parties without a previous relationship with the specialists, however indirect, will often find it hard to receive full, personal service."[21]

In the People's Republic of China, which has a tiny judiciary relative to its substantial population, laws and social norms are enforced at the neighborhood level through residents' committees and neighborhood organizations. Victor Li observes that because there are so few trained specialists in law, "the Chinese legal system must, of necessity, be simple in structure, method, and content so that relatively untrained people or even members of the general public can play an active role in the legal process."[22] Neighborhood organizations, which utilize the services of more than one million lay mediators, resolve both civil and criminal matters by keeping watch over people's daily activities and by applying social pressure for conformity and cooperation.[23] Because people within a given neighborhood are likely to share the same economic status, issues of wealth discrimination are less likely to influence outcomes for most low-level disputes. This relative equality in the application of justice provides no lessons for the United States, however, because the Chinese system emphasizes significantly different values, including an extreme degree of supervision and control over daily life that would be unacceptable in American society. In addition, the abundance of trained legal professionals in the United States permits widespread use of formal judicial proceedings which can provide greater protection for individuals' rights.

Many communist countries have sought to place legal proceedings within the control of the citizenry by creating lay tribunals, or "workers' courts," which are frequently connected to a factory or apartment block. Theoretically, individuals can have disputes decided by their peers in these courts without the delays and costs associated with hiring legal professionals to pursue claims through formal judicial channels. In reality, not unlike small claims courts in the United States, the operation of these courts does not achieve its intended purpose. Workers' courts are primarily used by the government or factory managers to enforce rules and to punish workers for misbehavior.[24] The courts are not staffed by regular workers, and individuals rarely initiate grievances through the court process. These courts exhibit characteristics similar to those of some American alternative dispute-processing innovations. In both settings, legal structures were created to make dispute processing inexpensive and more accessible to the less affluent. In practice, however, the structures serve the purposes of established political interests by diverting burdensome claims and by creating new norm-enforcing mechanisms. As Robert Hayden has observed:

> One can, without being too cynical, see both the socialist idealization of social courts and at least one strand of American advocacy of alternative courts as resting on a desire to limit the kinds of external power available to individuals in their dealings with either other individuals

or corporate and government groups, thereby perpetuating the established power relationships within which those dealings take place.[25]

Criminal Justice

Poor people will not necessarily receive detrimental treatment in every conceivable judicial system. Because of its links with the political system, the judicial process will yield results that are influenced by the interests and ideologies of those who possess political and economic power within the governing system. Less affluent people are likely to suffer detrimental consequences, regardless of the form of the judicial system, simply because they lack the resources that permit affluent and organized interests to assert influence over political institutions, including the judiciary. If poor people controlled governing institutions, then affluent interests would probably suffer detrimental consequences in policy making and the judicial process.

The criminal justice system of the People's Republic of China provides an example of affluent individuals receiving discriminatory treatment in a judicial process. Under Mao, people who were considered members of the "enemy class," namely landlords, rich peasants, counterrevolutionaries, and rightists, received harsher punishments than other people for the same offenses.[26] This harsh treatment based upon social status reflected the political interests and ideology of the Communist Party leaders who dominated the Chinese governing system. In addition, government officials received favorable treatment by avoiding prosecution for a variety of offenses. This discrimination clashed with the stated principles of equality in Article 5 of the Organic Law of the People's Courts and Article 4 of the Criminal Procedure Law.[27] These provisions forbid discrimination by occupation, social origins, education, property status, and other personal characteristics. After Mao's death, the government initiated reforms to correct discriminatory abuses in the legal system. The government publicized criminal cases that were pursued against mid-level government officials and their relatives in order to prove that the new justice system would treat all people equally. Although reforms may have brought a reduction in discrimination based upon social status and an increase in the equitable application of laws to government officials, discriminatory attributes remain which reflect the distribution of political power. For example, no senior government officials have ever been prosecuted for economic crimes or corruption, a systemic problem which contributed to the Chinese student protest movement of 1989. As two experts on Chinese law have observed, "much remains to be done for the PRC to establish the credibility of the equality principle and to attack tigers and flies alike in applying criminal sanctions."[28]

Because the industrialized countries of Europe share many common characteristics with the United States, including democratic traditions, relatively affluent societies, and public acceptance of the legal system's legitimacy, these nations may provide the most useful comparisons on matters of equal justice.

The procedures used in many European criminal courts may diminish some risks of wealth discrimination. For example, instead of utilizing an American-style adversarial process, the West German courts employ an inquisitorial system.[29] The judge takes an active role in questioning witnesses and in seeking the facts rather than passively supervising the battle between the prosecutor and defense attorney. One of the significant problems affecting poor defendants in the United States is that their attorneys, who may be inexperienced or disinterested, are frequently mismatched against a professional prosecutor who can utilize the state's superior resources for investigation and presentation of evidence. This potential mismatch is ameliorated in Germany because the judge works actively as a neutral, authoritative actor to find the truth. Because Germany has professional judges who are trained specifically to become judges, are not former prosecutors or defense attorneys, and have secure positions, there are fewer explicit political pressures or sources of bias to affect their decisions. By contrast, because many judges in the United States are elected officials (whose views were shaped through prior experience as prosecutors), their discretionary decisions may yield discriminatory outcomes which favor the state over criminal defendants.

In addition, German prosecutors do not possess the broad discretionary authority of their American counterparts to determine charges, plea bargain, and recommend sentences. These significant discretionary powers of American prosecutors, who are under public pressure to obtain convictions as elected officials and advocates on behalf of the state, can foster harsh consequences for poor defendants. By contrast, according to Thomas Weigend, "German law casts the prosecutor in a more neutral position. He is to uphold the law, not simply seek a conviction."[30] Without the electoral politics and adversarial procedures that can encourage American prosecutors to seek convictions at all costs, the German system may permit prosecutors to assess cases more objectively.

In the nations of Western Europe, the potential severity of wealth discrimination is lessened because criminal sanctions are less harsh than they are in the United States. While the median prison sentence in the United States exceeds eight years and 17 percent of American prisoners are incarcerated for terms in excess of twenty years, criminal justice systems in Western Europe rarely incarcerate anyone for more than five years.[31] Unlike the United States, Western European countries have abolished capital punishment. As described in chapter 2, the discriminatory application of the death penalty places an especially difficult burden upon poor people who are represented by appointed counsel in the American judicial system. In Western Europe, discriminatory effects in the criminal justice system can cause the less affluent to receive a disproportionate percentage of the relatively short prison sentences imposed for a variety of serious offenses. In the United States, by contrast, discriminatory consequences can determine whether people spend decades or lifetimes in prison, or even whether they receive the death penalty unfairly.

The differences between the United States and the countries of Western Europe in regard to the severity of criminal sanctions can be attributed to several factors. First, many European countries still emphasize the rehabilitation of offenders. By contrast, the American system emphasizes punishment, in response to public dissatisfaction with crime rates. The inconsistent results of correctional rehabilitation programs have led to a trend toward emphasizing incapacitation and retribution as the primary purposes of criminal punishment within the United States.

A second factor encouraging harsher sentences in the United States is that American crime rates tend to be much higher than crime rates in Western European countries. In the late 1970s, aggravated assault rates in the United States were nearly three times greater than those in West Germany and robbery rates were more than six times greater.[32] Although the precise causes of crime are the subject of dispute, one notable difference between the United States and West Germany is frequently cited as contributing to the differential crime rates. Because West Germany protects its citizens with medical care and income-assistance programs that are most generous by American standards, the country does not have millions of desperately poor people. Whether due to frustration, social pressure, or choice, poor people in the United States comprise a substantial portion of the people who commit "street crimes."

A third factor influencing more severe criminal punishments in the United States is the level of violence involved in crimes within a country in which firearms are freely available. The message on a well-known poster distributed by an anti-handgun organization in the United States starkly portrays the prevalence of firearm violence: "In 1983, handguns killed 35 people in Japan[;] 8 in Great Britain[;] 27 in

Switzerland[;] 6 in Canada[;] 10 in Australia[;] and 9,014 in the United States."[33] The availability of handguns leads to more severe crimes because, unlike a criminal with a knife or club, a nervous or angry robber with a gun can initiate lethal outcomes with an unplanned, inadvertent, or accidental movement of one finger. The prevalence of violent crimes and the seriousness of injuries to crime victims in the United States reinforce the application of harsh criminal sanctions.

Sweden, West Germany, and other northern European countries frequently utilize a punishment, namely the "day-fine," intended to equalize the sanction placed upon affluent and poor offenders. A day-fine is a fine based upon the offender's income.[34] In punishing people with fines equal to a person's wages for a specified number of days, the burden of the fine is adjusted according to wealth. A wealthy person will pay larger fines for the same offense, but the fine will penalize the offender equally by confiscating the same percentage of income (e.g., twenty days pay) as that taken from a poorer person paying a smaller fine for that offense. For example, in Finland, a traffic fine of $11,400 was levied against a businessman earning $300,000 per year although a person with a modest income would only have paid $1,000.[35] In West Germany, fines are imposed in 83 percent of all criminal cases.[36] In the United States, one reason that fines are not as widely used is that poor offenders, many of whom are unemployed, infrequently employed, or substance abusers, cannot pay fines.[37] As one German scholar has noted, the lack of poverty in West Germany permits greater use of fines instead of incarceration as a criminal sanction: "Since the combined problem of crime and poverty does not exist in the Federal Republic in the same measure as in the United States, fines play an important role in the West German law of sanctions."[38]

Unlike correctional institutions in the United States, which isolate prisoners from the outside world and limit contacts between offenders and family members, many correctional institutions in Sweden and West Germany emphasize maintaining contacts between prisoners and the outside world. European correctional institutions stress the prisoner's reintegration into society. In addition to high-security prisons, Sweden and West Germany have "open prisons" designed to reduce the isolation experienced by offenders housed in traditional closed institutions.[39] Both countries also emphasize small, scattered institutions, educational release programs, and furloughs to enable prisoners to remain in contact with families and society.

The less harsh correctional procedures of Western Europe may not be possible in the United States because they reflect both a differing penal philosophy and a less burdensome population of violent offenders. In addition, American geography contributes to prisoners' isolation by making it difficult for poor people to visit incarcerated family members. In the United States, unlike European countries, which are small and have well-developed systems of public transportation, prisons are frequently located in isolated areas that are difficult to visit. For example, Washington state's maximum security prison at Walla Walla is located in the isolated southeastern corner of the state, hundreds of miles from the major population centers in the western portion of the state. Similarly, Michigan's maximum security facility at Marquette is located in the upper peninsula, hundreds of miles from the state's major cities in the south. Because poor families frequently face exceptionally difficult economic and personal pressures due to their financial status,[40] the American prison system, through its lengthy sentences and its isolation of offenders from society, may create especially deleterious consequences to the stability of less affluent prisoners' families. Such effects might be mitigated by utilizing the European system of scattering small prisons throughout the country and employing other mechanisms to facilitate family contacts.

Civil Litigation

One of the obvious problems within the American judicial process is the effect of unequal resources upon people's ability to utilize courts for processing disputes or for vindicating rights. Because of the costs associated with civil litigation, including money, time, and psychological perseverance, less affluent people face significant disadvantages when contemplating the use of civil litigation. European countries have addressed this problem through several mechanisms.

Great Britain's approach to equalizing civil justice is very similar to that of the United States.[41] Much like the Legal Services Corporation in the United States, Britain initiated its Legal Aid Scheme to provide legal assistance to people with little or no income. In addition, there are Community Law Centers in central cities and small-claims courts attached to county courts that provide increased access and advice for people with few resources. Underlying civil litigation in Britain, however, is a significant disincentive to initiating legal action. The losing party in British civil litigation must pay the costs of the opponent's lawyer. Although this policy would constitute a significant equalization mechanism in favor of the less affluent person who ultimately prevails in court, the inherent uncertainties in most legal disputes make this rule loom as a frightening deterrent to lawsuits. A poor person would have to think long and hard before undertaking such a risk by initiating a court action. Because the Legal Aid Scheme only aids the poorest people, people of modest means face the significant obstacles of securing legal counsel and paying court costs in order to sustain litigation until the hoped-for victory. Contingent fees are prohibited in Britain so there is little incentive for an attorney to accept cases without payment, even when the potential damage award may be substantial. In addition, legal aid programs in Britain, as well as in other European countries, share with their American counterparts the persistent problems of low attorney salaries, high personnel turnover, and heavy caseloads that detract from the quality of representation.[42] Thus Great Britain seems to provide few lessons for improving the American court system.

In West Germany, the courts can grant a provisional release from paying litigation costs in order to permit less affluent people to initiate litigation.[43] This release is based not only upon the court's assessment of the litigant's income and assets, but also upon an initial assessment of the prospects for success in the case. This preliminary evaluation of the merits of the case can lead to cautious decisions that deny fee waivers for potentially meritorious but highly uncertain claims. In addition, because the losing party in Germany pays all costs, including the opponent's attorneys' fees, all court costs, and fees for expert witnesses, even a modest claim can result in substantial fees for the loser. As in Britain, this rule serves as a deterrent to litigation, especially for the less affluent.

Germany's inquisitorial judicial process can foster equalizing effects, however, because judges bear substantial responsibility for fact-gathering. According to John Langbein, "Disparity in the quality of legal representation can make a difference in Germany, too, but the active role of the judge places major limits on the extent of the injury that bad lawyering can work on a litigant."[44] In German court proceedings, wealth and access to legal resources have less direct impact upon the outcome of cases because of the active role of the neutral, professional judge.

Italy, Portugal, and a few other countries have attempted to equalize civil justice by utilizing the so-called "charitable model" of assigning attorneys to represent low-income clients without compensation.[45] Not surprisingly, this system creates several significant problems. Lawyers shirk their responsibilities because uncompensated cases take time away from representation of paying clients. Representation for the poor is only provided for actual litigation. By contrast, affluent people can afford to pay for legal advice and information from attorneys while considering legal options prior to initiating lawsuits. In order to obtain legal aid, the poor person must submit a petition containing a statement about the facts in the case. This is a difficult task for people who have literacy problems or little education. In addition, the process of applying for representation disadvantages poor people by requiring them to reveal their cases before trial. This gives their opponents extra opportunities to prepare effective defense strategies. Moreover, poor claimants must survive a preliminary judgment on the merits of the case based upon their own unassisted presentations to the legal aid commission.[46] Poor people may find it difficult to make effective presentations to the commission, even in potentially meritorious cases.

The judicial system of the Soviet Union provides a mechanism for sharing the burden of representing clients who are too poor to pay legal fees. Because all legal fees are paid to a geographic collective to which all attorneys belong and lawyers are paid by the collective rather than by individual clients, lawyers assigned to represent poor people are paid the same as lawyers representing more affluent clients.[47] Thus, the income of every lawyer is modestly depressed to an equal degree by the free representation, and the more affluent clients effectively subsidize the legal work on behalf of the poor.

The Soviet legal system is not directly comparable to that of the United States. Soviet citizens lack both the substantive rights and the personal property which serve as the basis for civil litigation in the United States. Because people cannot accumulate property and wealth, Soviet civil cases concern relatively small amounts of money.[48] In addition, the legitimacy of the Soviet legal system is suspect because of the Communist party's historic stranglehold over governmental power. Despite these differences between the respective systems, the concept of sharing the burden of uncompensated representation among all attorneys presents one plausible method for increasing legal resources available to the poor.

In the American context, however, because law firms are businesses which seek to maximize profits through competition with other law firms, there is little incentive to accept voluntarily any burden of representing the poor. Although there are continual discussions about instituting mandatory pro bono obligations for American attorneys, effective implementation of such requirements, as Earl Johnson has observed, would elicit "nearly insurmountable political opposition . . . to any statute which awarded government the necessary policing powers over the workload of the private legal profession."[49]

Two European countries have aggressively sought to provide

civil justice resources for less affluent people. In Sweden, the Legal Aid Act provides government financial assistance to ensure that less affluent people can obtain legal advice and assistance by paying modest, adjustable fees based upon their income and assets.[50] In the Netherlands, a liberal income threshold for free legal assistance makes nearly two-thirds of the working population eligible for such aid.[51] In fact, as many as 40 percent of civil cases in some years have been filed by people receiving free legal assistance from the government. Such programs require a significant governmental commitment to raise revenues and to expend resources on behalf of less affluent people. In Sweden and the Netherlands, these legal assistance programs are part of a larger societal emphasis upon policies designed to share each country's wealth among all of its citizens. These policies are based upon a redistributive philosophy that is not evident in the elements of the dominant American ideology; namely, individualism, private property, and limited government.[52]

The commitment of resources to make civil litigation accessible to less affluent people has not provided a complete solution to problems of equal justice in Sweden and the Netherlands. In the Netherlands, many "law shops" run by university students and young lawyers were established during the 1970s because of dissatisfaction with the government's free legal assistance program. These "law shops" provided advice to four times as many people as did the free legal assistance program. While the government's program emphasized civil litigation between private citizens, the "law shops" addressed poor people's greatest legal needs, namely, conflicts with the government itself over provision of housing, income assistance, and other social welfare benefits.[53] Thus, the growth and operations of the "law shops" served as evidence of the inadequacy of governmental programs which, despite their apparent generosity, did not accurately recognize societal needs.

Sweden places great emphasis upon alternative dispute-processing mechanisms as a means to provide greater access to justice without formal litigation. Thus the potential expense of their legal aid program is limited because disputes are channeled into other forums. Bryant Garth has labeled Sweden's dispute mechanisms as "most striking and innovative" because they have created, among other things, a Consumer Ombudsman, a Market Court, a Public Complaint Board, and a simplified small claims process.[54] Although these innovations provide forums for complaints, they are not necessarily effective in protecting the rights of less affluent people. For example, the Public Complaint Board possesses no authority to enforce its recommendations with civil or criminal sanctions and must instead hope for voluntary compliance by merely threatening the offending business or institution with adverse publicity.[55]

Conclusion

A review of court processes employed in other countries yields examples of mechanisms which might reduce detrimental judicial outcomes for the poor if applied in the United States. For example, the active role of the professional German judges who reduce the advantages possessed by affluent litigants, and the expansive legal aid programs in Sweden and the Netherlands illustrate two mechanisms that contribute to an increase in equal access to justice for poor people. It is highly unlikely that any such reforms from other countries would be adopted by the United States. The social conditions affecting individual citizens and the design of judicial processes are both linked to prevailing ideologies and political traditions within a country. As chapter 8 will discuss, American society is different from other societies in significant ways, which influence the existence of wealth discrimination and the possibilities for reform. Although courts in the United States possess the most constitutional authority to make policy decisions that will advance equality, in contrast to the equalization efforts of other industrialized countries, the distribution of legal resources and the application of discretionary judgments within the American judicial system strongly reinforce discriminatory outcomes affecting poor people.

CHAPTER EIGHT

Court Reform and Equal Justice

What are the prospects for achieving the aspirational ideal of "Equal Justice Under Law"? As discussed in the foregoing chapters, wealth discrimination and detrimental outcomes for the poor in the judicial system are fostered by a number of factors ranging from conscious value choices by Supreme Court justices to subtle interactions between defense attorneys and their clients. Because these factors are intimately linked to the interests and attitudes of authoritative actors who wield power over judicial outcomes, it would be difficult to initiate effective changes. Despite the obvious difficulties in attempting to reform any established governmental institution, especially one with so many decisions and interactions hidden from public view, it is still useful to consider what, if anything, might be done to reduce courts' unequal treatment of less affluent people.

Equalizing Civil Litigation

The United States has experimented with alternative forums to provide greater access to justice for less affluent citizens. Small-claims courts, Neighborhood Justice Centers and other innovations reduce threshold costs and the need for professional representation, but they do not necessarily provide equal justice. As discussed in chapter 3, there are significant risks that alternative mechanisms may become a means to coerce settlements, to divert poor people into less desirable forums, or to increase inadvertently the power of affluent actors.[1] Because the less affluent are more likely to be unaware of both their rights and the avenues for seeking redress for recognized claims, the creation of more accessible forums does not, in and of itself, ensure equalized access to disputes processing resources. As Guido Calabresi has concluded, "legal simplification, unless combined with aggressive and individualized seeking out of those who are 'unaware of their rights,' is unlikely to affect the most ignorant and disadvantaged."[2] The ability to recognize legal claims and to identify avenues to pursue them is associated with higher education and income levels. Thus disparities in educational attainment within American society, exacerbated by the patterns of unequal educational opportunity described in chapter 6, create a fundamental barrier to equalizing access to judicial resources.

Equalizing Resources

If judicial resources were distributed evenly across American society, many lawyers could devote their efforts to representation of the poor. Because more than 13 percent of Americans live below the government poverty level, 85,000 attorneys, constituting 13 percent of the bar, should hypothetically be working on behalf of the poor.[3] Some commentators believe that the poor generally have even greater needs for legal assistance than do middle-class people.[4] For example, a child custody hearing for a poor person may create additional legal issues concerning welfare eligibility. Thus, if the distribution of legal resources went according to need, more than 13 percent of American attorneys would work for the poor. In reality, only about 4 percent of attorneys work for legal aid or public defender programs.[5] How could legal resources be distributed more evenly to address the unmet needs of the poor?

Voluntary and mandatory pro bono programs are fraught with problems including powerful political opposition to their imposition upon the bar and questions about the quality of services that would be rendered to non-paying clients. Any increases in established government programs, such as the Legal Services Corporation, seem out of the question in an era of budget deficits. Other options requiring an increase in expenditures, such as a voucher program to permit government reimbursement of private attorneys selected by poor people themselves, seem equally unlikely.

The creation of any new government programs would probably require the identification of new sources of revenue support. One proposal to meet this need would be a sales tax upon legal services dedicated to increasing judicial resources for the poor.[6] Because legal services, especially those entailing substantial attorneys' fees, are primarily procured by affluent interests, such a tax would have a redistributive effect. The redistributive quality of such a tax could be ensured by creating a progressive sliding scale according to the wealth of the client or by limiting the tax to legal services charged at a rate above a certain threshold level. If a lawyer charged only $50 per hour and thereby presumably served primarily middle-class clients, such legal services may be exempt from the tax. Lawyers who charge more than $100 per hour would have the tax applied to their fees because they presumably serve a more affluent clientele. According to calculations for the 1970s, a 10-percent tax on legal services would have yielded revenues sufficient to fund civil legal representation for the poor at a level fifteen times greater than that actually supplied.[7] Although this program could clearly make more resources available for equal access to justice and could draw those resources primarily from the pockets of the individual and corporate entities who could best afford to pay, the control that affluent interests have over the design of tax policies makes such a program highly unlikely.[8]

Lois Forer, an experienced state judge and author of several books on flaws in the legal system, has offered several suggestions for reducing the discriminatory impact of judicial processes.[9] Judge Forer recommends that access fees, which sometimes bar the poor from court, be abolished. Instead, courts should utilize several factors in order to impose "costs that actually reimburse the court for the time spent on the trial"[10]

1. the actual cost of trial time expended on case;
2. the frivolous or substantial nature of claim;
3. delaying tactics in pretrial and trial periods;
4. the amount in issue in the case; and
5. the ability of the parties to pay.

This suggested method for allocating costs stems from a recognition that taxpayers subsidize the cost of litigation for all parties, including wealthy litigants. Although parties pay for their attorneys and other litigation expenses, they do not pay the costs for the time spent by judges and other court personnel in processing cases. Other than a filing fee, such as the $120 fee in federal district courts, taxpayers pick up the tab for most of the court's processing resources. This proposal aims to create "user's fees" for court proceedings based upon parties' ability to pay and the other listed factors.

Forer asserts that allocating costs in this manner could generate funds to pay attorneys to represent indigent claimants in civil, as well as criminal, cases. Forer also argues that these additional revenues from allocated court costs could be used to permit indigent litigants to select their own attorneys in both criminal and civil cases. Thus, the legitimacy of the judicial system would be enhanced because "[t]o force a poor litigant to be represented by an attorney he does not want and in whom he has little confidence significantly differentiates between the poor and the nonpoor and undermines the claim that the legal system provides equal justice to rich and poor."[11]

Would these proposals for increasing legal resources for the poor eliminate wealth discrimination within the judicial process? No. Although these suggestions would provide additional resources and increased representation for less affluent people, they constitute limited steps that do not fundamentally alter the causes of wealth discrimination. The values and interests of the elite judges and lawyers who make important discretionary decisions within the judicial system would still evince insensitivity to poverty. Because the composition of the judiciary is unaffected by such resource-oriented reforms, judges' decisions would still perpetuate established judicial policies that disadvantage poor people. For example, the Supreme Court's limited concern about wealth discrimination would not be altered. The views of the authoritative actors within the judiciary merely reflect societal ambivalence and insensitivity to issues of economic inequality. Piecemeal efforts to increase resources will not significantly alter the court processes and actors' interests which ultimately determine outcomes.

Although redistribution of legal resources does not constitute a complete solution for the numerous attributes of wealth discrimination within the court system, it is still desirable to reduce resource inequalities that limit access to justice. In a practical sense, however, there is no political constituency supporting efforts to equalize resources. As Judge Forer has observed, the legal community has limited its concern to merely urging the government not to cut the existing inadequate resources for providing representation for indigent people.[12] This limited support for legal aid represents a great shift from earlier decades in which lawyers opposed any governmental role. The relative weakness of this political support for equalizing legal resources is evident in the legal profession's underlying political interests. Richard Abel has identified political motivations and self-interest that underlie the legal profession's support for limited aid to the poor. Attorneys have pushed for government resources to be shifted from salaried legal aid attorneys to programs for reimbursing private attorneys for representing the poor. According to Abel, "The fear that state intervention would curtail professional autonomy seems to have evaporated in the face of potential economic benefits."[13]

Criminal Justice Reform

Because discriminatory attributes of the criminal justice system inequitably deprive less affluent people of their liberty, and even their lives, there are compelling reasons to seek reform of detrimental structures and processes. Although the adequacy of legal representation may be enhanced by increasing the resources available for dedicated, professional public defenders, the other influential aspects of the criminal justice system cannot be improved so readily.

For example, one factor influencing discriminatory applications is the police officer's discretion to arrest and press charges against particular individuals. In some contexts, police officers may utilize their discretion to deny the law's protection for poor people by, for example, refusing to arrest violent spouses in domestic disputes. Alternatively, police officers may discriminate against the poor through aggressive law enforcement tactics within less affluent communities, such as discretionary "stop and frisk" and arrest decisions that are influenced by negative stereotypes of poor people as criminals. There have been many efforts to increase control over police officers' discretionary decisions through training, professionalization, clarification of departmental procedures, and administrative decentralization for enhanced supervision. As Gary Sykes has demonstrated, however, these reforms have merely created an appearance of reform without actually controlling the discretion that is inherently possessed by officers who must make quick decisions while patrolling the streets.[14]

As discussed in chapter 2, discretionary authority is dispersed to actors throughout the criminal justice system. It is impossible to eliminate discretion in a system with so many decision makers influenced by scarce resources, personal interests, and exchange relationships. Some detrimental effects may be reduced by raising actors' consciousness about wealth discrimination within the system, but, in essence, discriminatory outcomes remain inevitable in a system infused with political attributes and discretionary decision making.

The decision on setting bail represents a significant decision point in the criminal justice process with broad detrimental consequences for poor defendants. Poor people who are unable to make bail due to their lack of money lose their freedom, become unemployed and unable to support their families, and subsequently suffer higher rates of conviction and harsher punishments. Innovative bail reform programs were implemented in many cities to permit release of poor defendants who might otherwise be confined to jail pending trial. Although these programs reduced racial discrimination in several cities,[15] as Malcolm Feeley has shown in regard to this and other reforms in the criminal justice system, there are significant problems in implementing, evaluating, and institutionalizing any significant changes in the judicial system.[16]

Most bail reform programs never receive permanent funding. They remain in a precarious position searching for grants and other funding sources every year. This financial instability affects the periodic evaluation process for reform programs because the evaluators frequently are supporters of the reforms and are determined to protect the programs. Thus, according to Feeley, the bail programs can "claim great success while having only marginal impact . . . [and] provide impressive records to funding agencies, which are not close enough to the subject to challenge evidence."[17] The autonomy of judicial actors and fragmented authority within the criminal justice system limit the possibilities for implementing effective reforms.

Inequality and Justice

Although the civil litigation reforms implemented in European countries do not provide a complete solution to the problems of unequal justice, other attributes of those societies reduce disparities between rich and poor. For example, while millions of Americans lack medical insurance, the countries of Western Europe universally supply basic medical care for their citizens. Thus, a less affluent person in the United States might literally be forced to choose between spending money for medical treatment and consulting a lawyer about a legal problem. In such instances, it would be no surprise if the person surrendered any hope of pursuing the legal claim. Similarly, European countries make greater efforts to provide housing, equal education, and income assistance to poorer people. Because less affluent people in the United States are consumed by a greater struggle to obtain the basic necessities of life, opportunities to expend resources in order to secure the benefits of the judicial process are an unaffordable luxury for many Americans.

The redistributive policies of many European countries mitigate the effects of wealth discrimination. By attempting to provide equality in fundamental services, these countries do not experience the same conflicts about education, housing, and access to civil justice that stem from American courts' unwillingness to apply the Equal Protection Clause to wealth discrimination. For example, Sweden utilizes its national taxation policies to advance social equality. In 1979, two six-person Swedish families making annual incomes of $4,600 and $23,000 respectively would have had identical net incomes of $14,117.[18] The tax system redistributes income through government benefits and services.

In the United States, by contrast, gross disparities in the distribution of wealth and income are an accepted aspect of American society. In 1980, the top fifth of income earners in American society took home nearly 41 percent of the country's after-tax income while the bottom fifth got less than 5 percent.[19] In regard to the country's total assets of real estate, corporate stock, and cash, the top 1 percent of American society controls nearly 25 percent of the nation's wealth.[20] In the mid-1980s, the American tax system became increasingly regressive and even less redistributive as the income tax rate for the wealthiest Americans was lowered.

Unlike the Europeans' philosophy of sharing the country's wealth with all citizens, American economic policy fosters inequality by distributing benefits to those possessing political power and by viewing the poor as responsible for their own circumstances. During the early 1980s, the United States moved toward a policy of contradictory treatment of rich and poor. As Thomas Byrne Edsall has demonstrated, the rich were rewarded with tax benefits as an incentive for increased economic productivity while incentives for the poor were based upon punitive policies:

> The dual process of cutting both taxes and social programs involved, however, a striking difference in the assumptions about motivations governing the behavior of the affluent and the poor. For those in the upper bracket, and for those managing corporate decision-making processes, . . . creation of new tax incentives would encourage more work, more investment, and more savings. . . . At the bottom end of the scale, the dominant assumption behind the social program cuts was precisely the opposite: the best way to achieve increased work is by making life tougher.[21]

Not suprisingly, the affluent voters who reaped the benefits from this approach were predominantly Republican supporters of the administration in power and the poor people who suffered the heaviest penalties were predominantly supporters of the Democrats.[22]

In sum, the acceptance of economic inequality in American society permeates the country's governing institutions and policies. The distribution of political and economic power ensures that economic inequality and attendant discriminatory effects will remain a fact of life in the courts and other governing institutions. Proposals to increase the judicial resources available to the less affluent would have limited mitigating effects upon the overall discriminatory consequences of court processes. When addressing problems confronting the poor, however, even modest proposals lack the necessary political constituency in Congress and in state legislatures to gain enactment and implementation.

Decisions made by actors in the court system that determine both individual outcomes and larger judicial policies reflect the dominant values and interests in American society. Thus, affluent people enjoy significant advantages in the judicial process while poor people suffer detrimental consequences that collide with the aspirational ideal of "Equal Justice Under Law." Fundamental reforms in the courts, and in other governing institutions, would require changes in prevailing social philosophies and the distribution of political power. Short of a massive redistribution of wealth through a Swedish-type tax system aimed at reducing the general resource disparities between rich and poor, the prospects for significantly altering the court system's discriminatory consequences for the poor remain dim. From the design of the criminal laws through the resource allocation policies for conducting civil and criminal litigation, the court system and its operating processes favor the interests of middle-class and affluent political majorities who control and comprise the decision makers in governmental institutions.

Within the past few decades, the expansion of constitutional rights for criminal defendants and the creation of limited legal representation programs for the poor have reduced some of the most blatant discriminatory consequences of the past. The trend toward equalizing access to justice for poor people during the 1960s came to a halt in the 1970s and 1980s as judicial and legislative decisions limited the available resources and programs. Although discrimination against poor people may not be a planned goal of the system, court processes continue to produce detrimental outcomes as an inevitable reflection of a society that accepts and expects gross disparities in political power and economic resources.

Notes

CHAPTER 1

1. "The Can't Do Government," *Time*, Oct. 23, 1989, pp. 28–32.

2. Harry P. Stumpf, *American Judicial Politics* (New York: Harcourt Brace Jovanovich, 1988), p. 42.

3. Lawrence Baum, *American Courts: Process and Policy* (Boston: Houghton Mifflin, 1986), pp. 5–7.

4. Bureau of the Census, *Poverty in the United States: 1987*, Series P-60, No. 163, Feb. 1989, p. 1.

5. Ibid.

6. Charles A. Murray, *Losing Ground: American Social Policy 1950–1980* (New York: Basic Books, 1984).

7. Bud Shuster, *Believing in America*, in *Poverty: Opposing Viewpoints*, ed. William Dudley (St. Paul, MN: Greenhaven Press, 1988), pp. 25–32.

8. "Homelessness," *Akron Beacon Journal*, Nov. 27, 1989, p. A10.

9. John McCormick and Peter McKillop, "The Other Suburbia: An Ugly Secret in America's Suburbs: Poverty," *Newsweek*, June 26, 1989, pp. 22–23.

10. Peter Passell, "Congress Debates Poverty Figures, But the Poor Don't Get Any Richer," *Akron Beacon Journal*, July 24, 1989, p. C7.

11. Bureau of the Census, *Poverty in the United States: 1987*, p. 157.

12. Bureau of the Census, *Money Income of Households, Families, and Persons in the United States: 1986*, Series P-60, No. 159, June 1988, p. 31.

13. Ibid., p. 75.

14. Ibid.

15. Bureau of the Census, *Poverty in the United States: 1987*, pp. 2, 7, 8.

16. Fred R. Harris and Roger W. Wilkins, eds., *Quiet Riots: Race and Poverty in the United States* (New York: Pantheon Books, 1988).

17. William J. Wilson, *The Declining Significance of Race* (Chicago, IL.: University of Chicago Press, 1978).

18. Ibid., p. 110.

19. See Norman C. Amaker, *Civil Rights and the Reagan Administration* (Washington, DC: Urban Institute Press, 1988); Lincoln Caplan, *The Tenth Justice* (New York: Vintage Books, 1987).

20. City of Richmond v. Croson Co., 109 S. Ct. 706 (1989) (program to reserve percentage of city contracts for minority-owned businesses found unconstitutional); Martin v. Wilks, 109 S. Ct., 2180 (1989) (parties outside of discrimination case permitted to challenge consent decree settling discrimination claims through new promotion program).

21. Wards Cove Packing Co. v. Atonio, 109 S. Ct. 2115 (1989) (limit use of statistical evidence to prove discriminatory employment practices); Patterson v. McLean Credit Union, 109 S. Ct. 2362 (1989) (civil rights statute limited to apply to hiring decisions but not discriminatory treatment in the workplace).

22. See Gilbert Ware, ed., *From the Black Bar: Voices for Equal Justice* (New York: Putnam's, 1976); Cassia Spohn, John Gruhl, and Susan Welch, "The Effect of Race on Sentencing: A Reexamination of an Unsettled Question," *Law and Society Review*, 16 (1981): 71–88.

23. "Equal Justice? Two Task Forces Raise Questions of Bias in the Courts," *Detroit Free Press*, Dec. 26, 1989, p. 6A.

24. McClesky v. Kemp, 107 S. Ct. 1756 (1987).

25. Stuart A. Scheingold, *The Politics of Rights: Lawyers, Public Policy, and Political Change* (New Haven, CT.: Yale University Press, 1974).

26. Abram Chayes, "The Role of the Judge in Public Law Litigation," *Harvard Law Review*, 89 (1976): 1281–1316.

27. Donald Horowitz, *The Courts and Social Policy* (Washington, DC: The Brookings Institution, 1977).

28. C. Neal Tate, "Personal Attribute Models of the Voting Behavior of U.S. Supreme Court Justices: Liberalism in Civil Liberties and Economics Decisions, 1946–1978," *American Political Science Review*, 75 (1981): 355–367; Sheldon Goldman, "Voting Behavior on the U.S. Courts of Appeals Revisited," *American Political Science Review*, 69 (1975): 491–506.

29. See Charles A. Johnson and Bradley C. Canon, *Judicial Policies: Implementation and Impact* (Washington, DC: Congressional Quarterly Press, 1984).

30. For an excellent review of social science studies concerning judicial decision making, see James L. Gibson, "From Simplicity to Complexity: The Development of Theory in the Study of Judicial Behavior," *Political Behavior*, 5 (1983): 7–49.

31. See Abraham S. Blumberg, "The Practice of Law as a Confidence Game: Organization Co-optation of a Profession," *Law and Society Review*, 1 (1967): 15–39; Christopher E. Smith, *The United States Magistrates in the Federal Courts: Subordinate Judges* (New York: Praeger, 1990).

32. See Terence P. Thornberry, "Race, Socioeconomic Status and Sentencing in the Juvenile Justice System," *Journal of Criminal Law and Criminology*, 64 (1973): 90–98; Stevens H. Clarke and Gary G. Koch, "The Influence of Income and Other Factors on Whether Criminal Defendants Go to Prison," *Law and Society Review*, 11 (1976): 57–92.

33. David O'Brien, "The Seduction of the Judiciary: Social Science and the Courts," *Judicature*, 63 (1980): 8–21; Lois Forer, *Money and Justice: Who Owns the Courts?* (New York: Norton, 1984), pp. 171–89.

34. Sheldon Goldman, "Reagan's Judicial Appointments at Mid-term: Shaping the Bench in His Own Image," *Judicature*, 66 (1983): 346.

35. Ibid.

36. Justice William Rehnquist, Speech at Louisiana State University, *New York Times*, May 16, 1983, p. A14, quoted in Forer, *Money and Justice*, p. 77.

37. Committee on the Judicial Branch, *Simple Fairness: The Case for Equitable Compensation of the Nation's Federal Judges* (Washington, DC: Judicial Conference of the United States, 1988), p. 31.

38. Chief Justice William Rehnquist, Press Conference, Washington, DC: Mar. 15, 1989 (from audio tape of C-SPAN broadcast).

39. Committee on the Judicial Branch, *Simple Fairness*, p. 64.

40. Bureau of the Census, *Money Income of Households*, p. 75.

41. "A Raise by Any Other Name," *Newsweek*, Nov. 27, 1989, p. 43.

42. Christopher E. Smith, "Federal Judicial Salaries: A Critical Appraisal," *Temple Law Review*, 62 (1989): 864.

43. See Beverly Blair Cook, "Sentencing Behavior of Federal Judges: Draft Cases—1972," *University of Cincinnati Law Review*, 42 (1973): 597–633; David J. Danelski, "Values as Variables in Judicial Decision-Making: Notes Toward a Theory," *Vanderbilt Law Review*, 19 (1966): 721–740; James L. Gibson, "Judges' Role Orientations, Attitudes and Decisions: An Interactive Model," *American Political Science Review*, 72 (1978): 911–924.

CHAPTER 2

1. Gunnar Myrdal, *An American Dilemma: The Negro Problem and Modern Democracy* (New York: Harper and Row, 1944), pp. 548–549.

2. Patricia Wald, "Poverty and Criminal Justice," Appendix C in Task Force on the Administration of Justice, *Task Force Report: The Courts* (Washington, DC: U.S. Government Printing Office, 1967), p. 151.

3. William J. Chambliss, *Crime and the Legal Process* (New York: McGraw-Hill, 1969), p. 86.

4. Richard J. Bonnie and Charles H. Whitebread II, *The Marihuana Conviction: A History of Marihuana Prohibition in the United States* (Charlottesville, VA: University Press of Virginia, 1974), p. 36.

5. Charles E. Silberman, *Criminal Violence, Criminal Justice* (New York: Vintage Books, 1978), p. 138.

6. Samuel Walker, *Sense and Nonsense about Crime*, 2d ed. (Pacific Grove, CA: Brooks/Cole, 1989), p. 238.

7. John Irwin, *The Jail: Managing Rabble in American Society* (Berkeley: University of California Press, 1985).

8. Among households with a family income below $7,500, 6.3 percent were victimized by violent crime and 7.3 percent were victimized by burglary in 1986. By contrast, the respective figures for households with family incomes exceeding $25,000 were 4.1 and 4.8 respectively. U.S. Department of Justice, *Bureau of Justice Statistics Bulletin*, "Households Touched by Crime in 1987," May 1988, p. 3.

9. The literature on causes of criminal behavior is reviewed extensively in James Q. Wilson and Richard J. Herrnstein, *Crime and Human Nature* (New York: Simon & Schuster, 1985). Although credited with a far-reaching review, Wilson and Herrnstein have been criticized for the conclusions which they drew from their survey of the field. Leon J. Kamin, "Is Crime in the Genes? The Answer May Depend on Who Chooses What Evidence" (book review), *Scientific American*, Feb. 1986, pp. 22–27.

10. For a description of the substantial harms to society caused by corporate actions, see, Ronald C. Kramer, "Is Corporate Crime Serious Crime? Criminal Justice and Corporate Crime Control," *Journal of Contemporary Criminal Justice*, 2 (June 1984): 2–10.

11. Robert M. Bohm, "Crime, Criminal and Crime Control Policy Myths," *Justice Quarterly*, 3 (1986): 201.

12. Walker, *Sense and Nonsense about Crime*, pp. 250–251.

13. Ibid., p. 21.

14. George F. Cole, *The American System of Criminal Justice*, 4th ed. (Monterey CA: Brooks/Cole, 1986), pp. 135, 138. Cole's work provides the basis for the presentation of the criminal justice system's underlying characteristics.

15. Ibid., p. 141.

16. Samuel Walker, " 'Broken Windows' and Fractured History: The Use and Misuse of History in Recent Police Patrol Analysis," *Justice Quarterly*, 1 (1984): 84.

17. Ibid.

18. Samuel Walker, *Popular Justice* (New York: Oxford University Press, 1980), p. 225.

19. Michael Lipsky, "Street-Level Bureaucracy and the Analysis of Urban Reform," *Urban Affairs Quarterly*, 6 (1971): 391–409.

20. Douglas A. Smith and Christy A. Visher, "Street-Level Justice: Situational Determinants of Police Arrest Decisions," *Social Problems*, 29 (1981): 174.

21. Ibid., p. 175.

22. Albert Reiss, *The Police and the Public* (New Haven, CT: Yale University Press, 1971), pp. 144–50.

23. Marvin Wolfgang, Robert M. Figlio, and Thorsten Sellin, *Delinquency in a Birth Cohort* (Chicago, IL: University of Chicago Press, 1972).

24. Terence P. Thornberry, "Race, Socioeconomic Status and Sentencing in the Juvenile Justice System," *The Journal of Criminal Law and Criminology*, 64 (1973): 90–98.

25. James Q. Wilson, *Thinking about Crime*, rev. ed. (New York: Basic Books, 1983), p. 83.

26. Jerome Skolnick, *Justice Without Trial: Law Enforcement in a Democratic Society*, 2d ed. (New York: Wiley, 1975), p. 48.

27. Wilson, *Thinking about Crime*, p. 97.

28. Elizabeth A. Stanko, "The Impact of Victim Assessment on Prosecutors' Screening Decisions: The Case of the New York County District Attorney's Office," in *Criminal Justice: Law and Politics*, ed. George F. Cole, 5th ed. (Pacific Grove, CA: Brooks/Cole, 1988), p. 173.

29. H. Richard Uviller, "The Unworthy Victim: Police Discretion in the Credibility Call," *Law and Contemporary Problems*, 47 (1984): 15–33.

30. Elinor Ostrom, "Equity in Police Services," in *Evaluating Performance of Criminal Justice Agencies*, ed. Gordon P. Whitaker and Charles David Phillips (Beverly Hills, CA: Sage, 1983), pp. 99–125.

31. See Roy B. Flemming, *Punishment Before Trial* (New York: Longman, 1982).

32. See Paul B. Wice, *Freedom for Sale: A National Study of Pretrial Release* (Lexington, MA: Lexington, 1974).

33. Malcolm M. Feeley, *The Process Is the Punishment* (New York: Russel Sage Foundation, 1979), pp. 199–243.

34. Herbert Jacob and James Eisenstein, "Sentences and Other Sanctions in the Criminal Courts of Baltimore, Chicago, and Detroit," in *Criminal Justice: Law and Politics*, ed. George F. Cole, 4th ed. (Monterey, CA: Brooks/Cole, 1984), p. 267.

35. Sotirios A. Barber, *On What the Constitution Means* (Baltimore, MD: Johns Hopkins University Press, 1984), p. 3.

36. Bell v. Wolfish, 441 U.S. 520 (1979).

37. William Landes, "Legality and Reality: Some Evidence in Criminal Procedure," *Journal of Legal Studies*, 3 (1974): 287–337 (effect on likelihood of conviction); Stevens H. Clarke and Gary G. Koch, "The Influence of Income and Other Factors on Whether Criminal Defendants Go to Prison," *Law and Society Review*, 11 (1976): 57–92 (effect on probability of prison sentence).

38. Forrest Dill, "Discretion, Exchange, and Social Control: Bail Bondsmen in Criminal Courts," *Law and Society Review*, 9 (1975): 644–674.

39. Malcolm M. Feeley, *Court Reform on Trial* (New York: Basic Books, 1983), pp. 40–79.

40. Bureau of Justice Statistics, *Profile of Jail Inmates: Sociodemographic Findings from the 1978 Survey of Inmates in Local Jails* (Washington DC: U.S. Government Printing Office, 1980), p. 6.

41. Bureau of Justice Statistics, *Correctional Populations in the United States, 1986* (Washington, DC: U.S. Government Printing Office, 1989), p. 6.

42. Irwin, *The Jail*.

43. Cole, *American System of Criminal Justice*, p. 360.

44. George F. Cole, "The Decision to Prosecute," *Law and Society Review*, 4 (1970): 313–343.

45. James Eisenstein and Herbert Jacob, *Felony Justice: An Organizational Analysis of Criminal Courts* (Boston, MA: Little, Brown, 1977), pp. 19–39.

46. Johnson v. Zerbst, 304 U.S. 458 (1938).

47. Powell v. Alabama, 287 U.S. 45 (1932).

48. Betts v. Brady, 62 S. Ct. 1252, 1257 (1942).

49. Gideon v. Wainwright, 372 U.S. 335 (1963).

50. Argersinger v. Hamlin, 407 U.S. 25 (1972).

51. Scott v. Illinois, 440 U.S. 367 (1979).

52. U.S. Department of Justice, *Bureau of Justice Statistics Bulletin,* "Criminal Defense for the Poor, 1986," Sept. 1988, pp. 3–4.

53. Robert L. Spangenberg, Beverly Lee, Michael Battaglia, Patricia Smith, A. David Davis, *National Criminal Defense Systems Study* (Washington, DC: Bureau of Justice Statistics, 1986), p. 35.

54. *Bureau of Justice Statistics Bulletin,* "Criminal Defense for the Poor, 1986," p. 6.

55. Robert Hermann, Eric Single, John Boston, *Counsel for the Poor: Criminal Defense in Urban America* (Lexington, MA: Lexington, 1977), p. 67.

56. Spangenberg et al., *National Criminal Defense Systems Study,* p. 36.

57. Smith v. State, 140 Ariz. 355 (1984).

58. Victoria L. Swigert and Ronald A. Farrell, "Normal Homicides and the Law," *American Sociological Review,* 42 (1977): 24–25.

59. Clarke and Koch, "The Influence of Income and Other Factors on Whether Criminal Defendants Go to Prison," p. 83.

60. Hermann, Single, and Boston, *Counsel for the Poor,* p. 153.

61. Johnathan D. Casper, "Did You Have a Lawyer When You Went to Court? No, I Had a Public Defender," *Yale Review of Law and Social Action,* 1 (1971): 4–9.

62. Ibid.

63. Roy B. Flemming, "Client Games: Defense Attorney Perspectives on Their Relations with Criminal Clients," *American Bar Foundation Research Journal* (1986): 253–277.

64. Hermann, Single, and Boston, *Counsel for the Poor,* p. 167.

65. Abraham S. Blumberg, "The Practice of Law as a Confidence Game: Organization Co-optation of a Profession," *Law and Society Review* (1967): 15–39.

66. Lynn M. Mather, "The Outsider in the Courtroom: An Alternative Role for Defense," in *Criminal Justice: Law and Politics,* 5th ed., ed. George F. Cole (Pacific Grove, CA: Brooks/Cole, 1988), pp. 253–270. By contrast, one researcher has argued that public defenders in Chicago are truly adversaries to the prosecutor. Lisa J. McIntyre, *The Public Defender: The Practice of Law in the Shadows of Repute* (Chicago, IL: University of Chicago Press, 1987), pp. 171–178.

67. Blumberg, "The Practice of Law as a Confidence Game," p. 30.

68. Glasser v. U.S., 315 U.S. 60 (1942).

69. Valerie P. Hans and Neil Vidmar, *Judging the Jury* (New York: Plenum Press, 1986), p. 54.

70. Ibid., p. 75.

71. James M. Gleason and Victor A. Harris, "Race, Socio-Economic Status, and Perceived Similarity as Determinants of Judgements by Simulated Jurors," *Social Behavior and Personality*, 3 (1975): 175–180; James M. Gleason and Victor A. Harris, "Group Discussion and Defendant's Socio-Ecomomic Status as Determinants of Judgments by Simulated Jurors," *Journal of Applied Social Psychology*, 6 (1976): 186–191. Another study found no significant discrimination: Robert I. Gordon and Paul D. Jacobs, "Forensic Psychology: Perception of Guilt and Income," *Perceptual and Motor Skills*, 28 (1969): 143–146.

72. John Hagan, "Extra-Legal Attributes and Criminal Sentencing: An Assessment of the Sociological Viewpoint," *Law and Society Review*, 8 (1974): 357–383.

73. Clarke and Koch, "The Influence of Income and Other Factors on Whether Criminal Defendants Go to Prison"; Alan J. Lizotte, "Extra-Legal Factors in Chicago's Criminal Courts: Testing the Conflict Model of Criminal Justice," *Social Problems* 25 (1978): 564–580; Swigert and Farrell, "Normal Homicides and the Law."

74. Lizotte, "Extra-Legal Factors in Chicago's Criminal Courts," p. 578.

75. Clarke and Koch, "The Influence of Income," p. 83.

76. Thornberry, "Race, Socioeconomic Status and Sentencing," p. 97.

77. Steven B. Boris, "Sterotypes and Dispositions for Criminal Homicide," *Criminology*, 17 (1979): 139–158.

78. Theodore G. Chiricos and Gordon P. Waldo, "Socioeconomic Status and Criminal Sentencing: An Empirical Assessment of a Conflict Proposition," *American Sociological Review*, 40 (1975): 753–772. This study was subsequently discussed in John Hagen and Kristin Bumiller, "Making Sense of Sentencing: A Review and Critique of Sentencing Research," *Research on Sentencing: The Search for Reform*," Vol. 2, eds. Alfred Blumstein, Jacqueline Cohen, Susan E. Martin, and Michael H. Tonry (Washington, DC: National Academy Press, 1983), pp. 14–15, Andrew Hopkins, "Is There a Class Bias in Criminal Sentencing?," *American Sociological Review*, 42 (1977): 176–177, and other articles.

79. Martin A. Levin, "Urban Politics and Policy Outcomes: The Criminal Courts," in *Criminal Justice: Law and Politics*, 5th ed., ed. George F. Cole (Pacific Grove, CA: Brooks/Cole, 1988), pp. 330–352.

80. McClesky v. Kemp, 107 S. Ct. 1756 (1987).

81. Ronald A. Farrell and Victoria L. Swigert, "Legal Disposition of Inter-Group and Intra-Group Homicides," *Sociological Quarterly*, 19 (1978): 565–576.

82. Robert Fitzgerald and Phoebe C. Ellsworth, "Due Process v. Crime Control: Death Qualification and Jury Attitudes," *Law and Human Behavior*, 8 (1984): 46.

83. Claudia C. Cowan, William C. Thompson, and Phoebe C. Ellsworth, "The Effects of Death Qualification on Juror's Predisposition to Convict and on the Quality of Deliberation," *Law and Human Behavior*, 8 (1984): 60, citing Reid Hastie, Steven D. Penrod, and Nancy Pennington, *Inside the Jury* (Cambridge, MA: Harvard University Press, 1983), p. 130.

84. William C. Thompson, Claudia L. Cowan, Phoebe Ellsworth, and Joan C. Harrington, "Death Penalty Attitudes and Conviction Proneness," *Law and Human Behavior*, 8 (1984): 95–113.

85. William J. Bowers, "The Pervasiveness of Arbitrariness and Discrimination Under Post-*Furman* Capital Statutes," *Journal of Criminal Law and Criminology*, 74 (1983): 1067–1100.

86. Murray v. Giarratano, 109 S. Ct. 2765 (1989), discussed in Linda Greenhouse, "Rights of Death Row Inmates to Legal Assistance Are Limited," *New York Times*, June 24, 1989, p. 8.

87. "From Tragedy to Travesty," *Newsweek*, Apr. 24, 1989, p. 68; "No Happy Ending," *Time*, Mar. 6, 1989, p. 56.

88. Ross v. Moffitt, 417 U.S. 600 (1974).

89. Thomas Y. Davies, "Gresham's Law Revisited: Expedited Processing Techniques and the Allocation of Appellate Resources," *Justice System Journal*, 6 (1981): 372–404.

90. Bounds v. Smith, 430 U.S. 817 (1977).

91. Falzerano v. Collier, 535 F. Supp. 800, 803 (D.N.J. 1982).

92. Christopher E. Smith, "United States Magistrates and the Processing of Prisoner Litigation," *Federal Probation*, 52 (1988): 13–18.

93. William B. Turner, "When Prisoners Sue: A Study of Prisoner Section 1983 Suits in the Federal Courts," *Harvard Law Review* 92 (1979): 610–663; Roger A. Hanson, "What Should Be Done When Prisoners Want To Take The State To Court?" *Judicature*, 70 (1987): 223–227.

94. Feeley, *Court Reform on Trial*, pp. 40–79.

95. Walker, *Sense and Nonsense about Crime*, pp. 70–71.

CHAPTER 3

1. Robert H. Mnookin and Lewis Kornhauser, "Bargaining in the Shadow of the Law: The Case of Divorce," *Yale Law Journal*, 88 (1979): 950–997.

2. Joel B. Grossman and Austin Sarat, "Access to Justice and the Limits of Law," *Law & Policy Quarterly*, 3 (1981): 131.

3. Marc Galanter, "Reading the Landscape of Disputes: What We Know and Don't Know (and Think We Know) About Our Allegedly Contentious and Litigious Society," *U.C.L.A. Law Review*, 31 (1983): 4–71.

4. Richard E. Miller and Austin Sarat, "Grievances, Claims, and Disputes: Assessing the Adversary Culture," *Law and Society Review*, 15 (1980–81): 544.

5. Galanter, "Reading the Landscape of Disputes," pp. 17–18.

6. Ibid., pp. 14–15.

7. Suzanne R. Thomas-Buckle and Leonard G. Buckle, "Doing unto Others: Disputes and Dispute Processing in Urban American Neighborhood," in *Neighborhood Justice: Assessment of an Emerging Idea*, eds. Roman Tomasic and Malcolm M. Feeley (New York: Longman, 1982), pp. 78–90.

8. Frances K. Zemans, "Legal Mobilization: The Neglected Role of Law in the Political System," *American Political Science Review*, 77 (1983): 698–699.

9. Philip R. Lochner, Jr., "The No Fee and Low Fee Legal Practice of Private Attorneys," *Law and Society Review*, 9 (1975): 443.

10. Harry P. Stumpf, *American Judicial Politics* (New York: Harcourt Brace Jovanovich, 1988), p. 234.

11. Henry R. Glick, *Courts, Politics, and Justice*, 2d ed. (New York: McGraw-Hill, 1988), p. 126.

12. Stewart Macaulay, "Lawyers and Consumer Protection Laws," *Law and Society Review*, 14 (1979): 115–171.

13. Miller and Sarat, "Grievances, Claims, and Disputes," p. 544.

14. Jerome R. Corsi, *Judicial Politics: An Introduction* (Englewood Cliffs, NJ: Prentice-Hall, 1984), p. 215.

15. Ibid., p. 216.

16. Stumpf, *American Judicial Politics*, p. 265.

17. United States v. Kras, 409 U.S. 434 (1973).

18. Ortwein v. Schwab, 410 U.S. 656 (1973).

19. Gayle Binion, "The Disadvantaged Before the Burger Court: The Newest Unequal Protection," *Law & Policy Quarterly*, 4 (1982): 46.

20. Lois G. Forer, *Money and Justice: Who Owns the Courts?* (New York: W.W. Norton, 1984), p. 97.

21. Gerald M. Stern, *The Buffalo Creek Disaster* (New York: Vintage Books, 1976).

22. Glick, *Courts, Politics, and Justice*, p. 127.

23. Marc Galanter, "Afterward: Explaining Litigation," *Law and Society Review* 9 (1975): 347. See also Marc Galanter, "Why the 'Haves' Come Out Ahead: Speculations on the Limits of Legal Change," *Law and Society Review*, 9 (1974): 95–160.

24. Barbara Yngvesson and Patricia Hennessey, "Small Claims, Complex Disputes: A Review of the Small Claims Literature," *Law and Society Review*, 9 (1975): 219–274.

25. Stumpf, *American Judicial Politics*, pp. 297–298.

26. Herbert Jacob, *Debtors in Court: The Consumption of Government Services* (Chicago, IL: Rand McNally, 1969), pp. 73–86.

27. Yngvesson and Hennessey, "Small Claims, Complex Disputes," pp. 269–271.

28. Howard S. Erlanger, Elizabeth Chambliss, and Marygold S. Melli, "Participation and Flexibility in Informal Processes: Caution From the Divorce Context," *Law and Society Review*, 21 (1987): 585–604.

29. Ralph C. Cavanagh and Deborah L. Rhode, "The Unauthorized Practice of Law and Pro Se Divorce: An Empirical Analysis," *Yale Law Journal*, 86 (1976): 104–184.

30. Stumpf, *American Judicial Politics*, p. 308.

31. Roman Tomasic, "Mediation as an Alternative to Adjudication: Rhetoric and Reality in the Neighborhood Justice Movement," In *Neighborhood Justice: Assessment of an Emerging Idea*, eds. Roman Tomasic and Malcolm M. Feeley (New York: Longman, 1982), p. 229.

32. Richard L. Abel "The Contradictions of Informal Justice," in *The Politics of Informal Justice*, Vol. 1, ed. Richard L. Abel (New York: Academic Press, 1982), pp. 267–320.

33. Christine B. Harrington, *Shadow Justice: The Ideology and Institutionalization of Alternatives to Court* (Westport, CT: Greenwood Press, 1985), p. 173.

34. Studies of these various ADR techniques in the federal courts are contained in: Kathy L. Shuart, *The Wayne County Mediation Program in the Eastern District of Michigan* (Washington, DC: Federal Judicial Center, 1984); E. Allan Lind and John E. Sheppard, *Evaluation of Court-Annexed Arbitration in Three Federal District Courts* (Washington, DC: Federal Judicial Center, 1983); M. Daniel Jacoubovitch and Carl M. Moore, *Summary Jury Trials in the Northern District of Ohio* (Washington, DC: Federal Judicial Center, 1982).

35. Dissenting Views of the Hon. Elizabeth Holtzman, U.S. Congress, House Report No. 1364, Magistrates Act of 1978, 95th Cong., 2d Sess., 1978, p. 42.

36. Christopher E. Smith, "Assessing the Consequences of Judicial Innovation: U.S. Magistrates' Trials and Related Tribulations," *Wake Forest Law Review*, 23 (1988): 455–490.

37. Forer, *Money and Justice: Who Owns the Courts?*, p. 108.

38. David Margolick, "Required Work for Poor Urged for Lawyers," *New York Times*, July 11, 1989, p. A1.

39. William Falsgraf, "President's Page: Access to Justice in 1986," *American Bar Association Journal*, 72 (Feb. 1986): 8.

40. Dorothy L. Maddi and Frederic R. Merrill, *The Private Practicing Bar and Legal Services for Low-Income People* (Chicago, IL: American Bar Association, 1971).

41. Mallard v. U.S. District Court, 104 L. Ed. 318 (1989) discussed in Linda Greenhouse, "Law on Free Legal Service Narrowed," *New York Times*, May 2, 1989, p. 8.

42. Joel F. Handler, Ellen J. Hollingsworth, and Howard Erlanger, *Lawyers and the Pursuit of Legal Rights* (New York: Academic Press, 1978), pp. 91–110.

43. Stern, *Buffalo Creek Disaster*, p. 298.

44. Lochner, "The No Fee and Low Fee Legal Practice of Private Attorneys," pp. 448–449.

45. Nan Aron, *Liberty and Justice for All* (Boulder, CO: Westview Press, 1989), pp. 80–82.

46. See Harry P. Stumpf, *Community Politics and Legal Services* (Beverly Hills, CA: Sage, 1975).

47. Corsi, *Judicial Politics: An Introduction*, p. 236.

48. Mark Kessler, *Legal Services for the Poor: A Comparative and Contemporary Analysis of Interorganizational Politics* (Westport, CT: Greenwood Press, 1987), p. 143.

49. Corsi,*Judicial Politics: An Introduction*, p. 243.

50. Kessler, *Legal Services for the Poor*, pp. 148–149.

51. Aron, *Liberty and Justice for All*, pp. 47–48, 122–130.

52. See Charles A. Johnson and Bradley C. Canon, *Judicial Policies: Implementation and Impact* (Washington, DC: Congressional Quarterly, 1984).

53. Kessler, *Legal Services for the Poor*, p. 150 n.12.

54. Jack Katz, *Poor People's Lawyers in Transition* (New Brunswick, NJ: Rutgers University Press, 1982), p. 182.

55. Ibid., pp. 185–186.

CHAPTER 4

1. Simon v. Eastern Kentucky Welfare Rights Organization, 96 S. Ct. 1917 (1976).

2. Lyng v. International Union, UAW, 108 S. Ct. 1184 (1988).

3. James V. Calvi and Susan Coleman, *American Law and Legal Systems* (Englewood Cliffs, NJ: Prentice-Hall, 1989), p. 195.

4. Goldberg v. Kelly, 90 S. Ct. 1011 (1970).

5. Calvi and Coleman, *American Law and Legal Systems*, pp. 196–197.

6. Ibid., p. 197.

7. Mathews v. Eldridge, 96 S. Ct. 893 (1976).

8. Ibid., at 910 (Brennan, J., dissenting).

9. Ortwein v. Schwab, 93 S. Ct. 1172 (1973).

10. Ernest Gellhorn and Barry Boyer, *Administrative Law and Process* (St. Paul, MN: West, 1981), p. 177.

11. Ibid., p. 178, citing Jerry L. Mashaw, "The Supreme Court's Due Process Calculus for Administrative Adjudication in *Mathews v. Eldridge*: Three Factors in Search of a Theory of Value," *University of Chicago Law Review*, 44 (1976): 28–59.

12. Richard L. Abel, "The Crisis Is Injuries, Not Liability," in *New Directions in Liability Law*, ed. Walter Olson (New York: Academy of Political Science, 1988, p. 36.

13. Donna P. Cofer, *Judges, Bureaucrats, and the Question of Independence* (Westport, CT: Greenwood Press, 1985), p. 5.

14. Albert H. Meyerhoff and Jeffrey A. Mishkin, "Application of *Goldberg v. Kelly*: Hearing Requirements to Terminate Social Security Benefits," *Stanford Law Review*, 26 (1974): 564.

15. Cofer, *Judges, Bureaucrats, and the Question of Independence,* p. 14.

16. Ibid., p. 9–13.

17. Ibid., p. 10.

18. Thomas C. Mans, "Selecting the 'Hidden Judiciary': How the Merit Process Works in Choosing Administrative Law Judges," *Judicature,* 63 (1979): 60–73; 130–143.

19. Cofer, *Judges, Bureaucrats, and the Question of Independence,* p. 12.

20. Ibid.

21. Susan G. Mezey, *No Longer Disabled: The Federal Courts and the Politics of Social Security Disability* (New York: Greenwood Press, 1988), pp. 95–120.

22. Jerry L. Mashaw, Charles J. Goetz, Frank I. Goodman, Warren F. Schwartz, Paul R. Verkuil, and Milton M. Carrow, *Social Security Hearings and Appeals: A Study of the Social Security Administration Hearing System* (Lexington, MA: Lexington Books, 1978), pp. 91–92.

23. William D. Popkin, "The Effect of Representation in Nonadversary Proceedings—A Study of Three Disability Programs," *Cornell Law Review,* 62 (1977): 989–1048.

24. Mashaw et al., *Social Security Hearings and Appeals,* p. 95.

25. Ibid., p. 94.

26. M.H. Schwartz, Commentary, "Adjudication Process Under U.S. Social Security Disability Law: Observations and Recommendations," *Administrative Law Review,* 32 (1980): 571.

27. Mashaw et al., *Social Security Hearings and Appeals,* p. 94.

28. Schwartz, "Adjudication Process Under U.S. Social Security Disability Law," pp. 561–565.

29. Donald E. Griffith Jr., "Administrative Law Judges in the Social Security Administration: An Examination of the Disability Determination Process," unpublished paper, Department of Political Science, University of Akron, 1988, p. 31.

30. Ibid., p. 30.

31. Cofer, *Judges, Bureaucrats, and the Question of Independence,* p. 140.

32. Mashaw et al., *Social Security Hearings and Appeals,* p. 122.

33. Cofer, *Judges, Bureaucrats, and the Question of Independence,* p. 97.

34. Ibid., pp. 94–98.

35. Chrisopher E. Smith, *United States Magistrates in the Federal Courts: Subordinate Judges* (New York: Praeger, 1990), pp. 175–177.

36. Ibid.

37. Mezey, *No Longer Disabled,* pp. 86–87.

38. Cofer, *Judges, Bureaucrats, and the Question of Independence,* p. 117; Gregory Spears, "200,000 Win Back Places on Disability Rolls," *Akron Beacon Journal,* Dec. 3, 1989, p. A3.

39. Mezey, *No Longer Disabled,* p. 133.

40. Ibid., p. 132.

41. Ibid., pp. 133–135.

42. Ibid., p. 178.

43. Ibid.

44. Daniel J. Baum, *The Welfare Family and Mass Administrative Justice* (New York: Praeger 1974), pp. 58–59.

CHAPTER 5

1. Brown v. Board of Education, 347 U.S. 483 (1954).

2. Swann v. Charlotte Mecklenburg Board of Education, 402 U.S. 1 (1971).

3. Miranda v. Arizona, 384 U.S. 436 (1966) (informing defendants of their rights); Gideon v. Wainwright, 372 U.S. 335 (1963) (right to counsel for indigent defendants).

4. Harry P. Stumpf, *American Judicial Politics* (New York: Harcourt Brace Jovanovich, 1988), p. 46.

5. For a description of the backgrounds of Supreme Court justices throughout history, see, Henry J. Abraham, *Justices and Presidents: A Political History of Appointments to the Supreme Court*, 2nd ed. (New York: Oxford University Press, 1985).

6. Felix Frankfurter, *Mr. Justice Holmes and the Supreme Court* (New York: Atheneum, 1965), p. 54.

7. James L. Gibson, "From Simplicity to Complexity: the Development of Theory in the Study of Judicial Behavior," *Political Behavior* (5) (1983): 32.

8. Ibid.

9. See David J. Danelski, "The Influence of the Chief Justice in the Decisional Process of the Supreme Court," in *American Court Systems*, eds. Sheldon Goldman and Austin Sarat (New York: Longman, 1989), pp. 486–499; Walter F. Murphy, *Elements of Judicial Strategy* (Chicago, IL: University of Chicago Press, 1964); C. Neal Tate, "Personal Attribute Models of the Voting Behavior of U.S. Supreme Court Justices: Liberalism in Civil Liberties and Economic Decisions, 1946–1978," *American Political Science Review*, 75 (1981): 355–367.

10. Harold J. Spaeth, *An Introduction to Supreme Court Decision Making*, rev. ed. (San Francisco, CA: Chandler, 1972), p. 65.

11. Harrell R. Rodgers, Jr. and Michael Harrington, *Unfinished Democracy: The American Political System* (Glenview, IL: Scott, Foresman, 1981), pp. 109–110.

12. Charles A. Beard, "Framing the Constitution," in *American Government: Readings and Cases*, 8th ed., ed. Peter Woll (Boston, MA: Little, Brown, 1984), pp. 35–36.

13. See Forrest McDonald, *We the People: The Economic Origins of the Constitution* (Chicago, IL: University of Chicago Press, 1958).

14. James Madison, "Federalist 10," in Woll, *American Government: Readings and Cases*, pp. 190–192.

15. Ibid., p. 191.

16. Michael Parenti, *Democracy for the Few*, 5th ed. (New York: St. Martin's Press, 1988), p. 66.

17. Luther v. Borden, 48 U.S. (7 How.) 1 (1849).

18. Dred Scott v. Sandford, 60 U.S. (19 How.) 393 (1857).

19. The Slaughterhouse Cases, 83 U.S. (16 Wall.) 36 (1873).

20. Plessy v. Ferguson, 163 U.S. 537 (1896).

21. Civil Rights Cases of 1883, 109 U.S. 3 (1883).

22. Muller v. Oregon, 208 U.S. 412 (1908) (working hours for women in Oregon limited to ten hours per day); Bunting v. Oregon, 243 U.S. 426 (1917) (ten-hour workday plus overtime provision covering men in Oregon).

23. Stephen L. Wasby, *The Supreme Court in the Federal Judicial System*, 3rd ed.(Chicago, IL: Nelson-Hall, 1988), p. 79.

24. Sheldon Goldman, *Constitutional Law: Cases and Essays* (New York: Harper and Row, 1987), pp. 304–305.

25. Hammer v. Dagenhart, 38 S.Ct. 529 (1918).

26. Ibid., at 534 (Holmes, J., dissenting).

27. Lochner v. New York, 25 S.Ct. 539 (1905).

28. Ibid., at 546.

29. Morehead v. Tipaldo, 298 U.S. 587 (1936).

30. Archibald Cox, *The Court and the Constitution* (Boston, MA: Houghton Mifflin, 1987), p. 128.

31. Ibid.

32. Ibid., p. 136.

33. West Coast Hotel v. Parrish, 300 U.S. 379 (1937).

34. United States v. Carolene Products Company, 304 U.S. 144 (1938).

35. In one exceptional case, the Court utlilized the Equal Protection Clause to strike down discrimination against Chinese people in San Francisco. Yick Wo v. Hopkins, 118 U.S. 356 (1886).

36. Goesaert v. Cleary, 335 U.S. 464 (1948).

37. Edwards v. California, 314 U.S. 160 (1941).

38. Graham v. Richardson, 403 U.S. 365 (1971).

39. In re Griffiths, 413 U.S. 717 (1973).

40. Foley v. Connelie, 98 S. Ct. 1067 (1978).

41. Levy v. Louisiana, 391 U.S. 68 (1968); Weber v. Aetna Casualty & Surety Co., 406 U.S. 164 (1972).

42. Labine v. Vincent, 401 U.S. 532 (1971).

43. Frontiero v. Richardson, 411 U.S. 671 (1973).

44. Craig v. Boren, 429 U.S. 190 (1976).

45. Griffin v. Illinois, 351 U.S. 12 (1956).

46. Harper v. Virginia Board of Elections, 383 U.S. 663 (1966).

47. Shapiro v. Thompson, 394 U.S. 618 (1969).

48. McDonald v. Board of Election Commissioners, 349 U.S. 802, 807 (1969).

49. San Antonio Independent School District v. Rodriguez, 93 S. Ct. 1278 (1973).

50. Ibid.

51. Ibid., at 1287.

52. Joel B. Grossman and Richard S. Wells, *Constitutional Law and Judicial Policy Making*, 3d ed. (New York: Longman, 1988), p. 402.

53. Robert Bennett, "The Burger Court and the Poor," in *The Burger Court: The Counter Revolution That Wasn't*, ed. Vincent Blasi (New Haven, CT: Yale University Press, 1983), pp. 46–61.

54. Michael W. McCann, "Equal Protection for Social Inequality: Race and Class in Constitutional Ideology," in *Judging the Constitution: Critical Essays on Judicial Lawmaking*, eds. Michael W. McGann and Gerald L. Houseman (Glenview, IL: Scott, Foresman, 1989), pp. 251–254.

55. Ibid., p. 253.

56. Ibid., p. 252.

57. Ibid.

58. Cox, *The Court and the Constitution*, pp. 311–316.

59. William Lasser, *The Limits of Judicial Power: The Supreme Court in American Politics* (Chapel Hill: University of North Carolina Press, 1988), pp. 246–272.

60. Harry P. Stumpf, *Community Politics and Legal Services* (Beverly Hills, CA: Sage, 1975), pp. 276–277.

61. Lawrence Baum, *The Supreme Court*, 3d ed. (Washington, DC: Congressional Quarterly Press, 1989), p. 92.

62. David M. O'Brien, *Storm Center: The Supreme Court in American Politics* (New York: Norton, 1986), p. 209.

63. Anthony Lewis, *Gideon's Trumpet* (New York: Vintage Books, 1964).

64. Wasby, *Supreme Court in the Federal Judicial System*, p. 153.

65. Mary Ann Harrell, *Equal Justice Under Law: The Supreme Court in American Life*, rev. ed. (Washington, DC: Foundation of the Federal Bar Association, 1975), p. 113.

66. Robert A. Dahl, *Democracy in the United States: Promise and Performance*, 4th ed. (Boston, MA: Houghton Mifflin, 1981), p. 161.

67. Ibid., p. 162.

CHAPTER 6

1. Lawrence Baum, *American Courts: Process and Policy* (Boston, MA: Houghton Mifflin, 1986).

2. Grove City College v. Bell, 465 U.S. 555 (1984).

3. U.S. Constitution, Art III.

4. See J. Woodford Howard, *Courts of Appeals in the Federal Judicial System* (Princeton, NJ: Princeton University Press, 1981).

5. Spallone v. United States (1990), cited in Linda Greenhouse, "Yonkers Councilmen's Fines Voided," *New York Times*, Jan. 11, 1990, p. 10.

6. See Jim Luther, "It's a Tax-Free Country for the Privileged Few: IRS Says Rich Get Advantage of Legal Breaks," *Akron Beacon Journal*, Oct. 22, 1989, p. A9.

7. Stuart Scheingold, *The Politics of Rights: Lawyers, Public Policy, and Political Change* (New Haven, CT: Yale University Press, 1974).

8. Charles Mohr, "Decisions on Bias Prompt Criticism," *New York Times*, June 13, 1989, p. 9; Aaron Epstein, "Reagan Appointee Pushes Top Court to Right," *Akron Beacon Journal*, June 11, 1989, p. G1.

9. Stuart Scheingold, "Constitutional Rights and Social Change: Civil Rights in Perspective," in *Judging the Constitution: Critical Essays on Judicial Lawmaking*, eds. Michael W. McCann and Gerald L. Houseman (Glenview, IL: Scott, Foresman, 1989), p. 80.

10. Frances Fox Piven and Richard A. Cloward, *Poor People's Movements: Why They Succeed; How They Fail* (New York: Vintage Books, 1977).

11. Powell v. Alabama, 287 U.S. 45 (1932).

12. Betts v. Brady, 316 U.S. 455 (1942).

13. Griffin v. Illinois, 76 S. Ct. 585 (1956).

14. Ibid., at 590.

15. Burns v. Ohio, 360 U.S. 252 (1959) (no filing fees required of indigent defendants wishing to appeal); Smith v. Bennett, 365 U.S. 708 (1961) (no filing fees for indigent defendants in state post-conviction proceedings).

16. Gideon v. Wainwright, 372 U.S. 335 (1963).

17. Archibald Cox, *The Court and the Constitution* (Boston, MA: Houghton Mifflin, 1987), p. 248.

18. Argersinger v. Hamlin, 407 U.S. 25 (1972).

19. Escobedo v. Illinois, 378 U.S. 478 (1964).

20. Douglas v. California, 372 U.S. 353 (1963).

21. Ross v. Moffitt, 94 S. Ct. 2437, 2446 (1974).

22. Ibid., at 2444.

23. Scott v. Illinois, 99 S. Ct. 1158 (1979).

24. Ibid., at 1162.

25. Ibid., at 1168–1169.

26. Boddie v. Connecticut, 91 S. Ct. 780 (1971).

27. United States v. Kras, 93 S. Ct. 631 (1973).

28. Ibid., at 644.

29. Ortwein v. Schwab, 93 S. Ct. 1172 (1973).

30. Ibid., at 1175.

31. Gayle Binion, "The Disadvantaged Before the Burger Court: The Newest Unequal Protection," *Law & Policy Quarterly*, 4 (1982): 46–47.

32. Lucius J. Barker and Twiley W. Barker, Jr., *Civil Liberties and the Constitution* (Englewood Cliffs, NJ: Prentice-Hall, 1986), pp. 541–542.

33. Fuentes v. Shevin, 92 S. Ct. 1983 (1972).

34. Mitchell v. W.T. Grant Company, 94 S. Ct. 1895 (1974).

35. Ibid., at 1914.

36. Ibid.

37. James S. Coleman, "The Concept of Equality of Educational Opportunity," in *Equal Education Opportunity* (Cambridge, MA: Harvard University Press, 1968), p. 14.

38. Quoted in Alan B. Wilson, "Social Class and Equal Opportunity," in *Equal Educational Opportunity* (Cambridge, MA: Harvard University Press), p. 81.

39. San Antonio Independent School District v. Rodriguez, 93 S. Ct. 1278 (1973).

40. Peter Irons, *The Courage of Their Convictions: Sixteen Americans Who Fought Their Way to the Supreme Court* (New York: Free Press, 1988), pp. 283–303.

41. San Antonio Independent School District v. Rodriguez at 1316 (Marshall, J., dissenting).

42. Robert W. Bennett, "The Burger Court and the Poor," in *The Burger Court: The Counter-Revolution That Wasn't*, ed. Vincent Blasi (New Haven, CT: Yale University Press, 1983), p. 55.

43. Patrick R. Hugg, "Federalism's Full Circle: Relief for Education Discrimination," *Loyola Law Review*, 35 (1989): 38.

44. Serrano v. Priest, 557 P.2d 929 (1976) (California); Robinson v. Cahill, 339 A.2d 193 (1975) (New Jersey).

45. Richard A. L. Gambitta, "Litigation, Judicial Deference, and Policy Change," *Law & Policy Quarterly*, 3 (1981): 141–165.

46. Howard LaFranchi, "School Tax Inequities Vex Texas," *Christian Science Monitor*, Sept. 9, 1988, p. 17.

47. Susan Tifft, "The Big Shift in School Finance," *Time*, Oct. 16, 1989, p. 48.

48. Donald W. Crowley, "Implementing Serrano: A Study in Judicial Impact," *Law & Policy Quarterly*, 4 (1982): 320.

49. Plyler v. Doe, 102 S. Ct. 2382 (1982).

50. Ibid., at 2398.

51. Ibid., at 2396.

52. San Antonio Independent School District v. Rodriguez at 1310.

53. Plyler v. Doe at 2408 (Burger, C.J., dissenting).

54. Ibid., at 2406 (Powell, J., concurring).

55. Ibid., at 2404 (Blackmun, J., concurring).

56. Milliken v. Bradley, 94 S. Ct. 3112 (1974).

57. Gary Orfield, *Must We Bus?: Segregated Schools and National Policy* (Washington, DC: Brookings Institution, 1978).

58. Lindsey v. Normet, 92 S. Ct. 862 (1972).

59. Ibid., at 874.

60. James v. Valtierra, 91 S. Ct. 1331 (1971).

61. Hunter v. Erickson, 89 S. Ct. 557 (1969).

62. Barker and Barker, *Civil Liberties and the Constitution*, p. 371.

63. Warth v. Seldin, 95 S. Ct. 2197 (1975).

64. Binion, "Disadvantaged Before the Burger Court," p. 49.

65. City of Eastlake v. Forest City Enterprises, Inc., 96 S. Ct. 2358 (1976).

66. Village of Arlington Heights v. Metropolitan Housing Development Corp., 97 S. Ct. 555 (1977).

67. Binion, "Disadvantaged Before the Burger Court," pp. 51–52.

68. Phillip J. Cooper, *Hard Judicial Choices: Federal District Court Judges and State and Local Officials* (New York: Oxford University Press, 1988), pp. 47–84.

69. Tom Hundley, "Bias Order Still in Effect in Parma," *Akron Beacon Journal*, Nov. 5, 1989, p. G1.

70. Bennett, "Burger Court and the Poor," p. 47–48.

71. Shapiro v. Thompson, 89 S. Ct. 1322 (1969).

72. Goldberg v. Kelly, 90 S. Ct. 1011 (1970).

73. Ibid., at 1017.

74. Ibid., at 1017, n. 8.

75. Dandridge v. Williams, 90 S. Ct. 1153 (1970).

76. Ibid., at 1161.

77. Wyman v. James, 91 S. Ct. 381 (1971).

78. Ibid., at 400 (Marshall, J., dissenting).

79. Califano v. Westcott, 99 S. Ct. 2655, 2661 (1979).

80. John Brigham, "Constitutional Property: The Double Standard and Beyond," in *Judging the Constitution: Critical Essays on Judicial Lawmaking*, eds. Michael W. McCann and Gerald L. Houseman (Glenview, IL: Scott, Foresman, 1989), pp. 187–204.

81. Roe v. Wade, 93 S. Ct. 705 (1973).

82. See Raymond Tatalovich, "Abortion: Prochoice Versus Prolife," in *Social Regulatory Policy: Moral Controversies in American Politics*, eds. Raymond Tatalovich and Byron W. Daynes (Boulder, CO: Westview Press, 1988), pp. 177–209.

83. Maher v. Roe, 97 S. Ct. 2376 (1977).

84. Ibid., at 2387 (Brennan, J., dissenting).

85. Webster v. Reproductive Health Services 109 S. Ct. 3040 (1989).

86. "Countdown: The Wars Within the States," *Newsweek*, July 17, 1989, p. 24.

CHAPTER 7

1. J. Woodford Howard, "Constitution and Society in Comparative Perspective," *Judicature*, 71 (1987): 114.

2. Broadus N. Butler, "The 1979 Constitution of the Federal Republic of Nigeria and the Constitution of the United States of America: A Historical and Philosophical Comparison," *Howard Law Journal*, 30 (1987): 1031.

3. Ibid., p. 115.

4. Constitution of the Union of Soviet Socialist Republics in *Constitutions of the Countries of the World*, Vol. 17, eds. Albert P. Blaustein and Gilbert H. Flanz (Dobbs Ferry, NY: Oceana Publications).

5. Article 52 of the Soviet Constitution guarantees freedom of con-

science for religious beliefs and Article 58 provides the right to lodge a complaint about the actions of government officials. Ibid.

6. The application of judicial review in the United States stems from Chief Justice John Marshall's opinion in Marbury v. Madison, 5 U.S. (1 Cranch) 137 (1803), which declared an act of Congress to be unconstitutional.

7. Louise I. Shelley, *Lawyers in Soviet Work Life* (New Brunswick, NJ: Rutgers University Press, 1984), p. 3.

8. Mauro Cappelletti and William Cohen, *Comparative Constitutional Law* (Indianapolis, IN: Bobbs-Merrill, 1979), p. 22.

9. Gary K. Bertsch, Robert P. Clark, and David M. Wood, *Comparing Political Systems; Power and Policy in Three Worlds*, 3rd ed. (New York: Wiley, 1986), p. 156.

10. Howard, "Constitution and Society in Comparative Perspective," pp. 113–114.

11. Archibald Cox, *The Court and the Constitution* (Boston, MA: Houghton Mifflin, 1987), pp. 377–378.

12. Lawrence M. Friedman, *Total Justice* (Boston, MA: Beacon Press, 1985).

13. Harry P. Stumpf, *American Judicial Politics* (New York: Harcourt Brace Jovanovich, 1988), p. 237.

14. Hiroshi Wagatsuma and Arthur Rosett, "The Implications of Apology: Law and Culture in Japan and the United States," *Law and Society Review*, 20 (1986): 461–498.

15. Setsuo Miyazawa, "Taking Kawashima Seriously: A Review of Japanese Research on Japanese Legal Consciousness and Disputing Behavior," *Law and Society Review*, 21 (1987): 219–241.

16. John O. Haley, "The Myth of the Reluctant Litigant," *Journal of Japanese Studies*, 4 (1978): 359, cited in Miyazawa, "Taking Kawashima Seriously," p. 222.

17. Marc Galanter, "Reading the Landscape of Disputes: What We Know and Don't Know (and Think We Know) about Our Allegedly Contentious and Litigious Society," *U.C.L.A. Law Review*, 31 (1983): 59.

18. Ibid.

19. Joel Rosch, "Institutionalizing Mediation: The Evolution of the Civil Liberties Bureau in Japan," *Law and Society Review*, 21 (1987): 243–266.

20. Miyazawa, "Taking Kawashima Seriously," p. 234.

21. Ibid.

22. Victor H. Li, *Law Without Lawyers: A Comparative View in China and the United States* (Boulder, CO: Westview Press, 1978), p. 10.

23. Ibid., pp. 44–61.

24. Yugoslavia is the only country in which workers make substantial use of the court for making claims against others. In that country, however, the workers' courts have evolved into formal judicial proceedings, with claimants represented by lawyers and judges trained in law. Robert M. Hayden, "Popular Use of Yugoslav Labor Courts and the Contradiction of Social Courts," *Law and Society Review*, 20 (1986): 229–251.

25. Ibid., p. 246.

26. Shao-Chuan Leng and Hungdah Chiu, *Criminal Justice in Post-Mao China* (Albany, NY: State University of New York Press, 1985), pp. 21, 104.

27. Ibid.

28. Ibid., p. 108.

29. Thomas Weigend, "Sentencing in West Germany," *Maryland Law Review* (1983): 37–89.

30. Ibid., p. 52.

31. Todd R. Clear and George F. Cole, *American Corrections* (Monterey, CA: Brooks/Cole, 1986), p. 107.

32. Joachim Herrmann, "Federal Republic of Germany," in *Major Criminal Justice Systems*, eds. George F. Cole, Stanislaw J. Frankowski, and Marc G. Gertz (Beverly Hills, CA: Sage, 1981), p. 88.

33. "God Bless America" poster, Handgun Control, Inc., Washington, DC.

34. Alvar Nelson, "Sweden," in *Major Criminal Justice Systems*, eds. George F. Cole, Stanislaw J. Frankowski, and Marc G. Gertz (Beverly Hills, CA: Sage, 1981), p. 117.

35. Matti Huuhtanen, "Finnish Speeders' Fines Fit Purses," *Detroit News*, Dec. 26, 1989, p. 2B.

36. Herrmann, "Federal Republic of Germany," p. 97.

37. George F. Cole, "Innovations in Collecting and Enforcing Fines," *NIJ Reports* [National Institute of Justice], July/Aug. 1989, pp. 3, 5.

38. Herrmann, "Federal Republic of Germany," p. 97.

39. Ibid., p. 105; Nelson, "Sweden," p. 128.

40. Mark G. Arnold and Greg Rosenbaum, *The Crime of Poverty* (Skokie, IL: National Textbook, 1973), pp. 20–22.

41. I. H. Jacob, "Access to Justice in England," in *Access to Justice: A World Survey*, Vol. 1, eds. Mauro Cappelletti and Bryant Garth (Milan: Giuffre, 1978), pp. 419–478.

42. Richard Abel, "Law Without Politics: Legal Aid Under Advanced Capitalism," *U.C.L.A. Law Review*, 32 (1985): 513–516, 581.

43. Rolf Bender and Christoph Strecker, "Access to Justice in the Federal Republic of Germany," in *Access to Justice*, Vol. 1, eds. Mauro Cappelletti and Bryant Garth (Milan: Giuffre, 1978), pp. 527–577.

44. John Langbein, "The German Advantage in Civil Procedure," in *Readings on Adversarial Justice: The American Approach to Adjudication*, ed. Stephan Landsman (St. Paul, MN: West, 1988), p. 63.

45. Earl Johnson, Jr., "Thinking about Access: A Preliminary Typology of Possible Strategies," in *Access to Justice*, Vol. 3, eds.,Mauro Cappelletti and Bryant Garth (Milan: Giuffre, 1978), p. 151.

46. Ibid., p. 151 n. 371.

47. Ibid., p. 150.

48. V. K. Puchinsky, "Access to Justice in the Soviet Union," in *Access to Justice*, Vol. 1, ed. Mauro Cappelletti and Bryant Garth (Milan: Giuffre, 1978), p. 820.

49. Johnson, "Thinking about Access," p. 154.

50. Per Olof Bolding, "Access to Justice in Sweden," in *Access to Justice*, Vol. 1, eds. Mauro Cappelletti and Bryant Garth (Milan: Giuffre, 1978), pp. 892–893.

51. J. C. Houtappel, "Access to Justice in Holland," in *Access to Justice*, Vol. 1, eds. Mauro Cappelletti and Bryant Garth (Milan: Giuffre, 1978), pp. 589–590.

52. Everett C. Ladd, *The American Polity*, (New York: Norton, 1987), pp. 59–60.

53. Houtappel, "Access to Justice in Holland," p. 592.

54. Bryant Garth, "The Movement Toward Procedural Informalism in North America and Western Europe: A Critical Survey," in *The Politics of Informal Justice*, Vol. 2, ed. Richard Abel (New York: Academic Press, 1982), p. 190.

55. Johnson, "Thinking about Access," p. 167.

CHAPTER 8

1. See Richard L. Abel, ed., *The Politics of Informal Justice* (New York: Academic Press, 1982).

2. Guido Calabresi, "Access to Justice and Substantive Law Reform: Legal Aid for the Lower Middle Class," *Access to Justice*, Vol. 3, eds. Mauro Cappelletti and Bryant Garth (Milan: Giuffre, 1978), p. 188.

3. Carol R. Silver, "The Imminent Failure of Legal Services for the Poor: Why and How to Limit Caseload," *Journal of Urban Law*, 46 (1969): 217–248.

4. Ibid., pp. 217–218.

5. Harry P. Stumpf, *American Judicial Politics* (New York: Harcourt Brace Jovanovich, 1988), p. 238.

6. Earl Johnson, "Thinking about Access: A Preliminary Typology of Possible Strategies," in *Access to Justice*, Vol. 3, eds. Mauro Cappelletti and Bryant Garth (Milan: Giuffre, 1978), pp. 154–155.

7. Ibid., p. 155.

8. For a discussion of how tax policies in the 1980s have increasingly favored affluent interests to the detriment of middle- and low-income people, see Thomas B. Edsall, *The New Politics of Inequality* (New York: Norton, 1984), pp. 202–242.

9. Lois G. Forer, *Money and Justice: Who Owns the Courts?* (New York: Norton, 1984), pp. 204–217.

10. Ibid., p. 206.

11. Ibid., p. 208.

12. Ibid., p. 207.

13. Richard L. Abel, "The Transformation of the American Legal Profession," *Law and Society Review*, 20 (1986): 12.

14. Gary W. Sykes, "The Functional Nature of Police Reform: The 'Myth' of Controlling the Police," *Justice Quarterly*, 2 (1985): 52–65.

15. Malcolm M. Feeley, *Court Reform on Trial* (New York: Basic Books, 1983), p. 71.

16. Ibid., pp. 191–207.

17. Ibid., p. 73.

18. "The Swedish Tax Revolt," *Wall Street Journal*, Feb. 1, 1979, p. 16.

19. Edsall, *New Politics of Inequality*, p. 221.

20. Ibid., p. 22.

21. Ibid., p. 227.

22. Ibid., p. 228.

Table of Cases*

*When the case name is not mentioned in the text, the reference is to the notes for each chapter from which the reader can refer to the appropriate place in the text.

Index

171